Grazing

*A Healthier Approach
to Snacks and Finger Foods*

Grazing

*A Healthier Approach
to Snacks and Finger Foods*

NATIONAL BESTSELLER

Julie Van Rosendaal

whitecap

Copyright © 2005 One Smart Cookie Inc.
Revised edition copyright © 2009 One Smart
Cookie Inc.
Whitecap Books

Whitecap Books is known for its expertise in the
cookbook market, and has produced some of
the most innovative and familiar titles found in
kitchens across North America. Visit our website at
www.whitecap.ca.

Copyedited by Andrea Lemieux
Proofread by Amelia Gilliland
Cover design by Setareh Ashrafologhalai
Interior design by John Vickers and Setareh
    Ashrafologhalai
Food photography and styling by Julie Van
    Rosendaal
Other photos by Julie Van Rosendaal

**Nutritional analyses have been calculated using
the Food Smart Business Edition. When a choice
is given, the analysis is based on the first listed
ingredient or quantity. Optional ingredients are
not included.**

Printed in China

Library and Archives Canada Cataloguing in
Publication

Van Rosendaal, Julie, 1970–

    Grazing : a healthier approach to snacks
and finger foods / Julie Van Rosendaal. -- Rev. and
updated

Includes index.
ISBN 978-1-55285-965-0

    1. Snack foods. 2. Appetizers. I. Title.

TX740.V35 2009   641.8'12   C2008-907497-1

The publisher acknowledges the financial support
of the Government of Canada through the Book
Publishing Industry Development Program (BPIDP)
and the Province of British Columbia through the
Book Publishing Tax Credit.

10 11 12 13 5 4 3 2

For Mom and Dad, grazers extraordinaire

Contents

Introduction

I like to eat. A lot.

I'm not the only one—food has always been culturally significant and eating an important social event, but in recent years it has become one of our favorite pastimes. We love to eat at home, at work, in the car, on the couch, at the movies, at school, and at every conceivable social gathering. All holidays revolve around food, and it's rare to be out of sight of a vending machine, coffee shop, convenience store, or drive-thru. It's no wonder 63 percent of us are overweight!

Our crazy schedules and love for food make snacking common and portable food hugely popular, whether we eat three meals a day like our moms taught us to or not. Many of us grab whatever might pass for breakfast on the way out the door. If you eat lunch anywhere but at home, you're either taking it with you or buying it somewhere. And who doesn't eat in the car? Everyone needs a little smackerel of something after work or school or before a workout. If you have kids, they require an almost constant supply of snacks. Then there are parties and social functions, that empty space beside your latte, and the absolute need to munch during a movie. Grazing has become our eating pattern of choice, and the good news is—doctors and nutritionists all over the world believe that it's the healthiest way to eat!

Eating several smaller meals and snacks over the course of the day (rather than two or three big ones) keeps your energy levels high and blood sugar levels on an even keel. And studies have shown that grazing also lowers your cholesterol, and consequently your risk of heart disease and stroke. Eating regularly also keeps your mind alert and hunger at bay, which will make you less likely to become ravenous and devour enough food to sustain an entire Boy Scout troop. (Not that I'd know from personal experience or anything.)

When you're hungry, you naturally crave energy-dense (read: high-calorie) foods, namely fat, which has more than double the calories of protein or carbs. When fat is combined with sugar or salt, it sure tastes good. And when fatty, sugary, salty snacks are so readily available, so cheap, so highly marketed, and so yummy, they're nearly impossible to resist. It's no wonder our best intentions crumble in the face of Whoppers, Krispy Kremes, and Ben & Jerry's! It's important that we make good grazing choices.

Studies have shown that people who skip meals or go for long periods of time without eating don't perform well, and that eating too little causes your metabolism to drop and your body to hold on to energy stores in response to the perceived famine. Conversely, big, heavy meals tend to slow us down—picture yourself lounging on the couch with your pants undone after a big turkey dinner. Our digestive system is similar to that of chimpanzees and gorillas, which nibble all day long and never overload on calories. (They also never outgrow their pants.) And eating more frequently throughout the day is natural for most kids, who have small stomachs but high energy requirements, so they need a steady fuel supply.

There's nothing better than sitting down to a good meal with family and friends, but the traditional three-square-meals-a-day schedule often encourages people to eat when they think they should, rather than when they're hungry. The recipes in this book can make balanced meals or just fill the gap any time of day and are perfect for sharing, which, after all, is the best part.

Now that our schedules are more hectic and mealtimes less rigid, our changing eating patterns make us lucrative targets for the snack, convenience, and fast-food industry, which spends billions of dollars annually to convince us we're busy (true) and don't have time to cook (not entirely true), so they can make life easier and less stressful for us (at what cost?). Snack foods, fast foods, and convenience foods tend to have the highest calorie content, the least nutritional value, and the most ingredients with names you can't even pronounce and that can't be categorized into a food group.

Because these kinds of products are so heavily marketed to kids, their health is suffering as well. It doesn't help when ad agencies pair junk food and soda with rock stars and cartoon characters to make them even more appealing to children. Guilt is a big selling tool for grownups: If you buy Hamburger Helper or go to McDonald's, you'll have more time to spend with your kids. But what better way to spend time together than cooking up from scratch something delicious? And consider the cost of convenience: When we choose fast food over healthy food (which can be just as fast), we prioritize convenience over health and money. The fact that opening a box or ordering takeout is a no-brainer also plays a role when we're stressed out, are tired, and don't have any fast and easy solutions. If we're willing to spend over $50 billion a year in an attempt to solve our weight issues, shouldn't we be willing to spend a little time? What is our well-being worth, and that of our families?

If you're a grazer, a party thrower, or an occasional snacker, this book is full of easy-to-prepare, portable, good-for-you, and, most importantly, delicious food that doesn't require a knife and fork. It provides ammo against the vending machine, comforts you when you need to relax, and feeds a crowd when your friends are over. This is real food you can take with you wherever you go, even if it's only as far away as the couch. And most of the recipes take less time than ordering a pizza. Eat up!

Got the Munchies?

One of the secrets of successful snacking is to keep hunger at bay by giving in to the munchies—during that midafternoon lull or in the evening in front of the TV. Most packaged foods that are intended to satisfy the munchies are a nutritional nightmare—they don't do much for you besides taste good, so it's best not to keep them in the house if you're like me and don't trust your self-control in their presence. Make sure your cupboard is loaded with healthy snacks or be prepared to stir up one of these fast recipes, and when you get the munchies you'll be doing your body a favor.

Just live by Miss Piggy's motto: Never eat more than you can lift.

Regular or Sweet Potato Oven Fries

Oven-baked fries are every bit as good as the deep-fried kind, and are cheap, fast, and easy to boot. Brightly colored sweet potatoes are among the most nutritious of all vegetables. Besides being much higher in fiber than regular potatoes, they are very high in beta-carotene, contain the carotenoids lutein and zeaxanthin, and supply substantial amounts of vitamins C and B6 and manganese. They are delicious roasted with garlic, oil, and chopped fresh rosemary. To make spicy ketchup for dipping, mix equal parts ketchup and salsa. This cuts the calorie content of ketchup, which contains more sugar than ice cream, almost in half!

1 Tbsp canola or olive oil (plus extra, if necessary)

3 medium russet or Yukon gold potatoes, unpeeled

OR

1 large sweet potato, peeled or unpeeled

1 garlic clove, crushed, or garlic powder to taste (optional)

salt or garlic salt and pepper to taste

Per serving:

Calories	114
Total fat	3.5 g
saturated fat	0.3 g
monounsaturated fat	2 g
polyunsaturated fat	1.1 g
Protein	2.5 g
Carbohydrates	18.8 g
Cholesterol	0 mg
Fiber	1.8 g
Calories from fat	27%

1   Oil a heavy rimmed baking sheet and put it in the oven; turn the oven on to 450°F.

2   Cut the potatoes into evenly sized wedges or into ½-inch-wide sticks. To draw out some of the starch, place them in a large bowl and cover with water; soak for 10 minutes. Drain the potatoes and thoroughly dry with paper towels or a tea towel.

3   Pull the hot baking sheet out of the oven and spread the potatoes in a single layer on it, flipping them around to coat a bit with the oil. Sprinkle with garlic (if using) and salt and pepper. Make sure they aren't crowded or overlapping or they will steam instead of brown properly.

4   Roast for about 20 minutes, turning once or twice, until golden and crisp. Serve immediately.

Serves 4.

SPICY CHILI CHEESE FRIES
Combine ¼ cup grated Parmesan cheese, 1 tsp chili powder, and ¼ tsp each garlic powder, salt, and pepper. Sprinkle the fries with the mixture on the baking sheet before baking.

SWEET & SPICY SWEET POTATO FRIES
Combine 1 Tbsp brown sugar, ½ tsp salt, a pinch of cayenne pepper, and a pinch of cinnamon. Sprinkle over the sweet potato fries as soon as they come out of the oven and toss until well coated and the heat of the potatoes partially melts the sugar.

Baked Potato Chips

Have you ever bought those high-end, thickly sliced olive oil potato chips at a gourmet shop for $6 per bag? Homemade potato chips are cheap and easy to make and can be seasoned however you like. Because they are baked with canola or olive oil, they are a good source of healthy mono- and polyunsaturated fats.

3 medium russet or Yukon gold potatoes, or 1 medium-large sweet potato, unpeeled

canola or olive oil, for cooking

1 garlic clove, crushed, or ½ tsp garlic powder (optional)

salt to taste

Per serving:

It's difficult to accurately gauge the nutritional value of this recipe, as it depends largely on the type of potato you choose, the amount of oil you use, and how much is actually absorbed by the potatoes; you can get away with using only a tablespoon or two of oil in total, if you're concerned with calories.

1 Preheat oven to 450°F.

2 Scrub the potatoes and slice lengthwise or widthwise into very thin, uniform slices. A mandolin does the best job. Try to get them about ⅛ inch thick.

3 If you are using crushed garlic or garlic powder, stir it into a small dish of oil. Drizzle 2 baking sheets with oil and place them in the oven to heat up for about 10 minutes.

4 Remove the baking sheets from the oven and arrange the potato slices on the sheets in a single layer. Bake until the potatoes are golden on the bottom side, about 15 minutes. Turn the potatoes over and bake until they are golden brown all over, about 10 minutes more.

5 Transfer to paper towels to cool and sprinkle with salt while they are still warm. Repeat with the remaining potatoes.

Serves 4–6.

Kettle Corn

Kettle corn is that salty-sweet popcorn you often find at farmers' markets. This version is a little more caramelly than regular kettle corn. It's really fast and easy to make when you need a caramel corn fix.

1 bag light butter-flavored microwave popcorn, popped

½ cup sugar

2 Tbsp water

1 tsp butter

Per serving:

Calories	200
Total fat	3.7 g
saturated fat	0.6 g
monounsaturated fat	3 g
polyunsaturated fat	0 g
Protein	2.1 g
Carbohydrates	40.7 g
Cholesterol	2.6 mg
Fiber	0 g
Calories from fat	16%

1 Place the popcorn in a large bowl. If you like, spray the bowl first with nonstick spray to keep it from sticking.

2 Combine the sugar, water, and butter in a small saucepan over medium heat. Bring to a boil, stirring constantly. Reduce heat to medium-low and simmer for 10 minutes, swirling the pan occasionally but not stirring, until the sugar is pale golden. Immediately pour over the popcorn and quickly stir to coat. Tongs work great for this.

3 Cool and eat. (It's usually cool enough for me by the time I get from the kitchen to the living room.)

Serves 4.

CHOCOLATE POPCORN

Once the sugar is golden, quickly stir in 2 Tbsp cocoa and pour over the popcorn, tossing to coat.

BANANA SPLIT POPCORN

Add 1 cup banana chips, ½ cup dried cherries, ½ cup peanuts, and ⅓ cup mini chocolate chips to the cooled popcorn.

Caramel Corn

There is no happier sight than a giant bowl of caramel corn—it's a good idea to have friends around to help you eat it. This version is far lower in fat than that made with a typical recipe.

A word about popcorn freshness: Each popcorn kernel contains a tiny amount of water that, when heated, causes pressure to build until the kernel turns itself inside out. Too many un-popped kernels is a sign that your stash has dried out. To prolong its life, store your kernels in an airtight container in the fridge or freezer.

8 cups air-popped popcorn (about ⅓ cup kernels)

½ cup roasted peanuts, almonds, pecans, or other nuts (optional)

1 cup packed brown sugar

½ cup corn syrup or liquid honey

2 Tbsp butter

1 tsp vanilla

¼ tsp baking soda

Per cup:

Calories	196
Total fat	2.9 g
saturated fat	1.6 g
monounsaturated fat	0.8 g
polyunsaturated fat	0.2 g
Protein	0.9 g
Carbohydrates	43.1 g
Cholesterol	6.9 mg
Fiber	1.1 g
Calories from fat	13%

1 Preheat oven to 250°F.

2 Spray a large bowl with nonstick spray and put the popcorn in it, along with the nuts if you're using them.

3 Combine the brown sugar, corn syrup, and butter in a medium saucepan and bring to a boil over medium heat. Boil without stirring, swirling the pan occasionally, for 4 minutes. Remove from heat and stir in the vanilla and baking soda. It will foam up at first.

4 Quickly pour over the popcorn and stir to coat well. Tongs work really well for this! Spread onto a baking sheet or roasting pan and bake for 30 minutes, stirring once or twice. Cool.

Makes about 9 cups.

CRACKER JACK
For caramel corn that tastes more like Cracker Jack, use half corn syrup and half dark molasses. Add ½ cup roasted peanuts as well.

BACON MAPLE CARAMEL CORN
WITH PECANS
Cook 3–4 slices of bacon until crisp; transfer to a plate and crumble. Use some of the drippings in place of the butter, and use maple syrup instead of the honey. Add pecans and the bacon at the same time.

Maple Pecan Caramel Corn

This is one of those snacks that I can't have at arm's reach or I'll likely polish off half the bowl. At Christmas I buy old mason jars and fill them with this popcorn to give away as gifts. Use more inexpensive grade B maple syrup if you like—it's fine for cooking with.

8 cups air-popped popcorn (about ⅓ cup kernels)

½ cup chopped pecans, toasted

1 cup pure maple syrup

2 Tbsp butter

¼ tsp salt

¼ cup dried cranberries (optional)

Per serving:

Calories	163
Total fat	4.3 g
saturated fat	2.5 g
monounsaturated fat	1.2 g
polyunsaturated fat	0.3 g
Protein	1.3 g
Carbohydrates	31 g
Cholesterol	10.4 mg
Fiber	1.6 g
Calories from fat	23%

1. Toss popcorn and pecans in a large bowl that has been sprayed with nonstick spray.

2. In a small saucepan, bring maple syrup, butter, and salt to a boil. Reduce heat and continue to boil for 15–20 minutes, until the mixture reaches 300°F (hard-crack stage) on a candy thermometer. If you don't have a candy thermometer, drizzle some of the syrup into ice water and it should separate into hard, brittle threads that break when bent.

3. Pour over the popcorn and quickly stir to coat completely. Stir in the cranberries if you're using them, and spread on a baking sheet to cool.

Serves 6.

Flavored Popcorn

Here are some great spice blends to add flavor to your popcorn. I find they won't stick to dry air-popped popcorn, so I like to sprinkle them over light-buttered microwave popcorn and shake it up in the bag while it's still warm. If you do it this way, you may want to eliminate the salt, since microwave popcorn is already salted. Otherwise, lightly butter your popcorn or spray it with oil from a spray bottle, which will distribute it lightly and evenly and give the spices something to stick to. Also try using prepared powdered dip mixes such as ranch and dill.

1 bag light-buttered microwave popcorn or several cups air-popped popcorn

Cajun

1 tsp sea salt (optional, if using plain unsalted popcorn)

1 tsp paprika

½ tsp garlic powder

¼ tsp black pepper

pinch cayenne pepper (optional)

Chili Cheese

2 Tbsp grated Parmesan cheese

1 tsp salt (optional, if using plain unsalted popcorn)

1 tsp chili powder

½ tsp ground cumin

Italian

2–4 Tbsp grated Parmesan cheese

1 tsp salt (optional, if using plain unsalted popcorn)

¼ tsp dried Italian seasoning

freshly ground black pepper to taste

Curry

1 tsp salt (optional, if using plain unsalted popcorn)

½ tsp curry powder

freshly ground black pepper to taste

Pesto

2 Tbsp grated Parmesan cheese

1 tsp dried basil, crushed

¼ tsp garlic powder

Party Mix

I know, party mix is kitschy. But I bet if someone put a bowl of it in front of you, you would eat some.

3 cups air-popped popcorn or light buttered microwave popcorn

3 cups Shreddies or Chex cereal

2 cups pretzel sticks

½ cup roasted peanuts, salted or unsalted

2 Tbsp melted butter or olive oil

1 Tbsp soy sauce

1 Tbsp Worcestershire sauce

1 Tbsp sugar

1 tsp lemon juice

½ tsp curry powder (optional)

½ tsp garlic salt

¼ tsp black pepper

pinch cayenne pepper

2–4 Tbsp grated Parmesan cheese (optional)

Per cup:

Calories	200
Total fat	7.3 g
saturated fat	2.3 g
monounsaturated fat	2.9 g
polyunsaturated fat	1.6 g
Protein	5.1 g
Carbohydrates	30.7 g
Cholesterol	6.9 mg
Fiber	3.4 g
Calories from fat	31%

1 Preheat oven to 300°F.

2 In a large bowl toss together the popcorn, cereal, pretzel sticks, and peanuts. In a small dish stir together the butter, soy sauce, Worcestershire sauce, sugar, lemon juice, curry powder (if you like), garlic salt, pepper, and cayenne. Drizzle over the cereal mixture and toss until evenly coated, then spread in a shallow roasting pan. If you like, sprinkle the lot with Parmesan cheese.

3 Bake for 45 minutes, stirring often, until toasted. Store extras in an airtight container.

Makes about 9 cups.

ASIAN PARTY MIX
Add a cup of wasabi peas to the dry mixture, and 2 tsp curry powder and ¼ tsp cumin to the seasonings.

My Granola

Homemade granola is a virtuous thing. It's cheap (compared with the store-bought variety), insanely easy to make, and low in saturated fat, and you can add any combination of fruit, nuts, and seeds to suit your taste. If you're a molasses fan, replace a few tablespoons of the honey or maple syrup with it. If you like coconut but not the fat it contains, add coconut extract instead of vanilla. Many recipes call for melted butter or oil, but I've discovered you don't need it, or miss it. However, if you'd like to boost your intake of healthy fats and omega-3s, add ¼ cup canola or flax oil to the honey–maple syrup mixture.

6 cups old-fashioned (large-flake) oats

1–2 cups chopped or sliced nuts and seeds (almonds, walnuts, pecans, green pumpkin seeds, pine nuts, sunflower seeds, ground flax seeds, or a combination)

¼ cup ground flax seeds (optional)

½ tsp cinnamon (optional)

¼ tsp salt

⅓–½ cup honey

⅓–½ cup maple syrup or brown rice syrup

¼ cup flax or canola oil (optional)

1 tsp vanilla, almond, or coconut extract (optional)

½–1 cup dried fruit, such as raisins, cran-berries, cherries, and blueberries, or chopped dried dates, apricots, apples, and pears

1   Preheat oven to 300°F.

2   In a large bowl, combine the oats, nuts and seeds, cinnamon (if you like), and salt. In a small bowl, stir together the honey, maple syrup, flax oil, and vanilla extract (or if you're not using oil and vanilla, don't bother mixing the honey and maple syrup first). Pour over the oats and toss to coat them well.

3   Spread the mixture on a large rimmed baking sheet and bake for 30–45 min-utes, stirring occasionally, until the mixture is golden. Remove from the oven and stir in the dried fruit. Let the granola cool completely on the baking sheet be-fore transferring to an airtight container or individual Ziploc bags to stash in your desk, car, or gym bag.

Makes about 8 cups.

Ground flax seeds, hulled green pumpkin seeds, sunflower seeds, pine nuts, pecans, walnuts, and sliced or slivered almonds all make great additions and add protein, fiber, vitamins, and minerals.

Per ⅓ cup:

Calories	221
Total fat	5.2 g
saturated fat	0.7 g
monounsaturated fat	2.4 g
polyunsaturated fat	1.6 g
Protein	7.5 g
Carbohydrates	37.6 g
Cholesterol	0 mg
Fiber	0.7 g
Calories from fat	21%

Another Granola

I've started breaking away from my usual granola routine and have another that's worth a try; I now can't decide which I like more, so I've included both. Brown rice syrup will create a crispier granola, but is far less sweet than honey, maple syrup, or sugar.

5 cups old-fashioned oats

2–3 cups almonds, pecans, hazelnuts, walnuts, or a combination

½ cup sesame seeds

¼ cup ground flax seeds

2 tsp ground cinnamon

1 tsp ground ginger

½ tsp salt

½ cup unsweetened applesauce (or a lunch box snack pack)

¼ cup maple syrup or brown rice syrup

¼ cup honey

2 Tbsp canola or flax oil

½–1 cup raisins, cranberries, chopped dried apricots, or a combination (optional)

1   Preheat the oven to 300°F.

2   In a large bowl, combine all of the dry ingredients. In a small bowl, stir together all of the wet ingredients. Pour the wet ingredients over the dry ingredients and stir well.

3   Spread out the mixture evenly onto 2 rimmed baking sheets. Bake for 35–40 minutes, stirring once or twice, until pale golden. Set aside to cool completely, then stir in the dried fruit, if you're adding some.

4   Store in airtight containers.

Makes 8–10 cups.

Per ⅓ cup:

Calories	212
Total fat	11 g
saturated fat	1.1 g
monounsaturated fat	5.5 g
polyunsaturated fat	3.9 g
Protein	6.1 g
Carbohydrates	24.3 g
Cholesterol	0 mg
Fiber	3.7 g
Calories from fat	45%

Spiced Nuts

Even though they are high in calories, nuts are also high in protein, fiber, vitamins, and minerals, so they make an excellent snack, so long as you exercise some restraint (portion control!). My friend Sue makes these addictive nuts all the time—in the oven they smell even better than potpourri.

1 Tbsp canola or olive oil or butter

1 garlic clove, finely crushed

2 tsp coarse sea salt or kosher salt

½ tsp ground cumin

½ tsp chili powder

¼ tsp ground ginger

¼ tsp cinnamon

pinch cayenne pepper

2 cups unsalted mixed nuts, such as pecans, walnuts, cashews, and almonds

Per ⅓ cup:

Calories	275
Total fat	26.7 g
saturated fat	2.3 g
monounsaturated fat	14.7 g
polyunsaturated fat	8.4 g
Protein	6.5 g
Carbohydrates	7 g
Cholesterol	0 mg
Fiber	3.1 g
Calories from fat	82%

1   Preheat oven to 300°F.

2   In a medium saucepan, combine the oil, garlic, salt, cumin, chili powder, ginger, cinnamon, and cayenne pepper over medium-low heat. Cook for a couple minutes, just until the spices become fragrant. Add the nuts and stir until well coated.

3   Spread the nuts out in a single layer on a rimmed baking sheet and bake for 20–25 minutes, shaking the pan occasionally, until fragrant and golden. Cool on the pan.

Makes 2 cups.

Meringue Nuts

These nuts are lightly coated with a layer of sweetened egg white, which can carry any flavor you like. Use white sugar instead of brown, or try maple sugar if you can get your hands on some.

1 large egg white

3 cups mixed nuts, such as pecans, walnuts, cashews, almonds, and hazelnuts

¼ cup packed brown sugar

1 tsp cinnamon

¼ tsp ground ginger

¼ tsp salt

pinch allspice

pinch nutmeg

Per ⅓ cup:

Calories	283
Total fat	24.2 g
saturated fat	1.9 g
monounsaturated fat	12.2 g
polyunsaturated fat	8.9 g
Protein	7.9 g
Carbohydrates	13.3 g
Cholesterol	0 mg
Fiber	2.5 g
Calories from fat	72%

1 Preheat oven to 300°F.

2 In a medium bowl, beat the egg white until foamy. Stir in the nuts, sugar, cinnamon, ginger, salt, allspice, and nutmeg.

3 Spread the mixture into a single layer on a baking sheet that has been sprayed with nonstick spray or lined with foil. Bake for 30 minutes, stirring occasionally, until golden. Cool on the pan.

Makes 3 cups.

Sweet Spiced Pecans

These make an insanely decadent snack, and they are unbelievable sprinkled onto a salad! Nuts are an excellent source of healthy mono- and polyunsaturated fats—the kind that lower your risk of heart disease—which makes these an excellent alternative to chips. Just remember that the same healthy fats are also high in calories, so keep portions moderate. Because they are substantial though, a small amount is satisfying.

2 Tbsp butter, melted, or canola or olive oil

1 Tbsp packed brown sugar

1 tsp balsamic vinegar

2 drops hot sauce (such as Tabasco)

1 Tbsp chopped fresh rosemary

½ tsp salt

¼ tsp freshly ground black pepper

2 cups pecan halves

1 Preheat the oven to 300°F.

2 Combine everything but the pecans in a medium bowl and stir well. Add the pecans and toss until well coated. Spread on a baking sheet.

3 Bake for 10–15 minutes, until golden.

Makes 2 cups.

Per ⅓ cup:

Calories	285
Total fat	28.3 g
saturated fat	4.3 g
monounsaturated fat	16.3 g
polyunsaturated fat	6.2 g
Protein	2.9 g
Carbohydrates	9.2 g
Cholesterol	10.4 mg
Fiber	2.4 g
Calories from fat	84%

Chewy Honey Energy Bars

Just like homemade cookies are far better than the packaged kind, homemade energy bars are better, and cheaper, than any granola bar you can buy at the store. Sunflower seeds are extremely nutritious, providing large quantities of protein, B vitamins, potassium, iron, and zinc. Both sunflower and sesame seeds are among the best food sources of vitamin E, and sesame seeds are also an exceptional source of calcium, iron, niacin, and folate.

3 cups Bran Flakes, Corn Flakes, or Raisin Bran cereal

½ cup hulled sunflower seeds, raw or toasted

½ cup sesame seeds, toasted

¼ cup sliced or slivered almonds, toasted

2 Tbsp flax seeds, ground (optional)

½ cup honey or Rogers' Golden Syrup

Per bar:

Calories	158
Total fat	7.4 g
saturated fat	0.8 g
monounsaturated fat	2.7 g
polyunsaturated fat	3.4 g
Protein	3.4 g
Carbohydrates	22.8 g
Cholesterol	0 mg
Fiber	2.8 g
Calories from fat	39%

1 Combine all the ingredients except the honey in a medium bowl that has been sprayed with nonstick spray.

2 Bring the honey to a boil in a small saucepan. Reduce the heat to low and simmer for about 8 minutes, until the honey reaches 275°F (soft-crack stage) on a candy thermometer. If you don't have a candy thermometer, pour a little of the hot syrup into ice water—it should separate into hard but pliable threads that bend slightly before breaking.

3 Pour over the cereal mixture and quickly stir to coat evenly.

4 Press the mixture into an 8- × 8-inch pan that has been sprayed with nonstick spray. Cool completely and cut into bars.

Makes 12 bars.

Sweet & Salty Granola-Nut Clusters

I used to bring granola bars and nuts along with me everywhere I went to fend off the temptation of fast food. Now I bring these clusters, which are sweet and salty, chewy and crunchy all at once. They are also an excellent source of protein, fiber, vitamins, and minerals. Use any combination of nuts and seeds you like—I usually buy an assortment from the bulk section of the grocery store.

1 cup mixed nuts and seeds: sliced or slivered almonds, pine nuts, chopped pecans or walnuts, hazelnuts, sunflower seeds, and pumpkin seeds all work well

½ cup sesame seeds

¼ cup ground flax seeds

¼ cup honey

2 Tbsp water

1 tsp canola or flax oil

1 cup low-fat granola (store-bought or recipe on page 11)

2 Tbsp sugar

1 tsp coarse sea salt

Per cluster:

Calories	163
Total fat	9.3 g
saturated fat	1.2 g
monounsaturated fat	4.4 g
polyunsaturated fat	3.1 g
Protein	3.9 g
Carbohydrates	18.4 g
Cholesterol	0 mg
Fiber	1.6 g
Calories from fat	48%

1 Preheat oven to 350°F.

2 Spread the nuts and seeds on a baking sheet and toast for 8–10 minutes, shaking often, until pale golden and fragrant. Set aside.

3 In a medium saucepan, combine the honey, water, and oil. Bring to a boil over medium heat. Stir in the nut mixture. Reduce heat to medium-low and cook, stirring, for another 2 minutes. Stir in the granola, sugar, and salt and cook for another minute.

4 Spread the mixture in a thick layer on a baking sheet and allow to cool. Once cooled, break into clusters, or squeeze it into balls while the mixture is still warm and pliable but cool enough to handle. Store extras in a tightly sealed container.

Makes about a dozen clusters.

Crackers & Crisps

Practically everyone bakes cookies, so why not crackers? Like cookies, they are far better homemade than store-bought. They are inexpensive and easy to make, and you can flavor them any way you like. Crackers are more than just vehicles for cheeses and dips—they make great snacks on their own. Try giving crackers to young kids instead of cookies to keep them happy. You'll feel better knowing you're not feeding them any additives or preservatives.

Basic Crackers

Everyone makes cookies at home, so why not crackers? This is a great basic cracker recipe to use as a blank canvas—experiment with different kinds of flour and flavorings such as herbs, spices, citrus zest, seeds, nuts, and grated sharp cheeses. To make sturdy tart shells, cut rolled cracker dough into rounds and press into mini muffin cups and bake until golden, then cool and fill with whatever you like.

2 cups flour: all-purpose, whole wheat, rye, oat, buckwheat, or a combination

1 tsp sugar

½ tsp salt

2 Tbsp butter, chilled

¾ cup water, milk, or buttermilk

any additions you like: coarse salt; sesame, poppy, fennel, or caraway seeds; dehydrated garlic; freshly ground pepper; Parmesan cheese; chopped fresh rosemary

Per cracker (plain):

Calories	23
Total fat	0.5 g
saturated fat	0.3 g
monounsaturated fat	0.1 g
polyunsaturated fat	0 g
Protein	0.5 g
Carbohydrates	4.1 g
Cholesterol	1.3 mg
Fiber	0.2 g
Calories from fat	20%

1 Preheat oven to 350°F.

2 Combine the flour, sugar, salt, and butter in the bowl of a food processor and pulse until well blended. Add the water or milk and pulse just until you have soft dough. (Alternatively, blend the butter into the flour mixture with a fork or your fingers, and stir in the liquid by hand.)

3 On a lightly floured surface, roll the dough out about ⅛ inch thick. Sprinkle with any flavorings you like, and roll gently with the rolling pin to help the toppings adhere.

4 Cut into squares, rectangles, or rounds with a pizza wheel, pastry cutter, cookie cutter, or knife, and transfer to an ungreased baking sheet. Reroll the scraps only once to get as many crackers as you can.

5 Bake for 15–20 minutes, until golden. Transfer to a wire rack to cool and store extras in a tightly sealed container.

Makes about 4 dozen crackers.

BUTTERMILK-CUMIN CRACKERS
Use half all-purpose and half whole wheat flour, add 1 tsp ground cumin to the mixture, and use buttermilk instead of water.

Flax Seed Wafers

Flax seeds are a great source of soluble and insoluble fiber, and are the best plant source of omega-3 fatty acids. It's important to mention, however, that because they are so teeny and hard they cannot be digested unless they are ground, so it's a good idea to give them a turn in a coffee mill or spice grinder before you use them. Store pre-ground flax in the fridge or freezer to prevent it from going rancid.

½ cup whole flax seeds

1 large egg

1 Tbsp olive or canola oil

2 Tbsp water

1 cup all-purpose or whole wheat flour

¼ tsp salt

coarse salt, for sprinkling (optional)

Per cracker:

Calories	59
Total fat	2.7 g
saturated fat	0.3 g
monounsaturated fat	1 g
polyunsaturated fat	1.2 g
Protein	1.9 g
Carbohydrates	7.1 g
Cholesterol	12 mg
Fiber	1 g
Calories from fat	40%

1 Preheat oven to 350°F.

2 Pulse the flax seeds in a coffee or spice grinder until broken up, but not finely ground (you want to have some texture in these). In a medium bowl, stir together the egg, oil, and water. Add the flour, salt, and ground flax seeds and stir until you have a stiff dough.

3 Pinch off 1-inch balls of dough and place them on a clean, dry, unfloured countertop. Roll with a rolling pin in one direction only (meaning up and down, not side to side, creating a sort of rustic oval), making them as thin as you can. They need to stick a bit to the countertop in order to achieve this—but you'll be able to peel them off afterward.

4 If you want them salty, sprinkle with coarse salt and roll slightly to help it adhere. Peel each off the counter and place on an ungreased baking sheet, spacing them about ½ inch apart. You will need to bake them in batches as they take up quite a bit of space on each sheet, but they don't spread at all.

5 Bake for 12–15 minutes, until golden and crisp.

Makes about 1½ dozen large crackers.

SESAME-PARMESAN CRACKERS
Add ¼ cup grated Parmesan cheese along with the flour, and substitute sesame seeds for the flax seeds.

Cheddar-Sesame Crackers

Whole wheat flour gives these a nutty flavor and adds fiber and antioxidants, but you could use all-purpose if you like. Old cheddar has a much more intense flavor than the medium or mild varieties, so you don't need as much of it.

1 cup whole wheat flour

½ cup grated old or extra-old cheddar cheese

pinch salt

2 Tbsp canola oil

½ cup water

sesame seeds, for sprinkling

Per cracker:

Calories	14
Total fat	0.8 g
saturated fat	0.2 g
monounsaturated fat	0.4 g
polyunsaturated fat	0.2 g
Protein	0.5 g
Carbohydrates	1.5 g
Cholesterol	0.5 mg
Fiber	0.3 g
Calories from fat	47%

1   Preheat oven to 375°F.

2   Combine the flour, cheese, and salt in the bowl of a food processor and pulse until well blended. Add the oil and pulse again. (Alternatively, use a fork or pastry blender in a regular bowl.) Add the water and pulse (or stir) until it looks well blended and crumbly.

3   Turn the mixture out onto a lightly floured surface and gather it into a ball. Roll the dough out about ⅛ inch thick; sprinkle with sesame seeds and roll again to help them adhere.

4   Cut into 1-inch squares with a pizza cutter or knife. Place on an ungreased baking sheet and prick each cracker with a fork. Bake for about 20 minutes, until golden.

Makes about 5 dozen 1-inch crackers.

CHEDDAR-PECAN CRACKERS
Omit the sesame seeds and add ½ cup finely chopped or ground pecans to the flour mixture.

Rosemary, Raisin & Pecan Crisps

I, along with practically everyone I know, have become voraciously addicted to the rosemary-pecan Raincoast Crisps by Lesley Stowe Fine Foods. The price tag (and my ability to down an entire box myself) convinced me to figure out how to make them on my own. It turns out the formula is similar to Boston brown bread. Voilà!

2 cups all-purpose flour

2 tsp baking soda

1 tsp salt

2 cups buttermilk

¼ cup brown sugar

¼ cup honey

1 cup raisins

½ cup chopped pecans

½ cup roasted pumpkin seeds (optional)

¼ cup sesame seeds

¼ cup flax seeds, ground

1 Tbsp chopped fresh rosemary

Per cracker:

Calories	30
Total fat	0.8 g
saturated fat	0.1 g
monounsaturated fat	0.4 g
polyunsaturated fat	0.3 g
Protein	0.7 g
Carbohydrates	5.3 g
Cholesterol	0.2 mg
Fiber	0.3 g
Calories from fat	23%

1 Preheat oven to 350°F.

2 In a large bowl, stir together the flour, baking soda, and salt. Add the buttermilk, brown sugar, and honey and stir a few strokes. Add the raisins, pecans, pumpkin seeds (if using), sesame seeds, ground flax seeds, and rosemary and stir just until blended.

3 Pour the batter into two 8- × 4-inch loaf pans that have been sprayed with non-stick spray. Bake for about 45 minutes, until golden and springy to the touch. Remove from the pans and cool on a wire rack.

4 The cooler the bread, the easier it is to slice really thin. You can leave it until the next day or pop it in the freezer. Slice the loaves as thin as you can and place the slices in a single layer on an ungreased baking sheet. (I like to slice and bake one loaf and pop the other in the freezer for another day.) Reduce the oven heat to 300°F and bake them for about 15 minutes, then flip them over and bake for another 10 minutes, until crisp and deep golden. Try not to eat them all at once.

Makes about 8 dozen crackers.

Rosemary, Rye & Raisin Crackers

Although I felt compelled to call these crackers, they aren't the kind that is conducive to scooping up dips. They are the kind you eat all by themselves, perhaps with a slice of cheddar cheese. Half-way between a cracker and a cookie, but very plain, they would be fantastic with a cheese tray. I love the crunchiness of the crackers with the chewiness of the raisins or figs.

1½ cups all-purpose flour

1 cup rye or whole wheat flour

2 Tbsp brown sugar

1 tsp baking powder

½ tsp salt

¼ cup butter, chilled

1–2 tsp fresh rosemary

½ cup water

1 cup raisins or chopped dried figs

Per cracker:

Calories	50
Total fat	1.2 g
saturated fat	0.7 g
monounsaturated fat	0.3 g
polyunsaturated fat	0.1 g
Protein	1 g
Carbohydrates	9.3 g
Cholesterol	3 mg
Fiber	0.8 g
Calories from fat	21%

1   Preheat oven to 350°F.

2   In the bowl of a food processor, combine flours, brown sugar, baking powder, and salt. Add the butter and rosemary and pulse until the mixture is well blended.

3   Transfer to a large bowl and add the water. Stir just until the dough comes together. Knead the dough gently a few times and then divide it in half.

4   Roll each piece out on a clean surface until it's about ⅛ inch thick and roughly the same size. Sprinkle one piece of dough evenly with raisins, lay the other piece on top, and roll it again to squish them together. Gently roll until it becomes one piece again, and you can pick it up and flip it over. Continue rolling until you have a large rectangle that is ¼ inch thick or thinner, and the raisins almost come through the surface. Cut into squares or rectangles with a pizza wheel or knife and transfer to an ungreased baking sheet.

5   Bake for 15–20 minutes, until pale golden around the edges. Transfer to a wire rack to cool.

    Makes 3½ dozen 1½- × 2-inch crackers.

Wheat Thins

These are really simple, plain crackers to make and to eat. Canola oil has the lowest concentration of saturated fat of all cooking oils, which makes these much healthier than the store-bought kind. It also has a neutral flavor—try substituting olive, walnut, or hazelnut oil for a nuttier, unique taste.

3 cups whole wheat flour (or half all-purpose and half whole wheat)

½ tsp salt

¼ cup canola or olive oil

1 cup water

coarse salt, for sprinkling (optional)

Per cracker:

Calories	18
Total fat	0.6 g
saturated fat	0 g
monounsaturated fat	0.3 g
polyunsaturated fat	0.2 g
Protein	0.5 g
Carbohydrates	2.7 g
Cholesterol	0 mg
Fiber	0.5 g
Calories from fat	30%

1   In a medium bowl, stir together the flour and salt. Add the canola oil and water and mix until you have a soft dough. Divide the dough in half and let it rest for about 15 minutes.

2   Preheat oven to 350°F.

3   On a lightly floured surface, roll the dough into a rectangle as thin as possible—no thicker than ⅛ inch. Sprinkle with salt (if you want to) and lightly roll to help it adhere.

4   Place the whole thing on an ungreased baking sheet and cut into squares with a pizza wheel or knife; don't bother to separate them. Prick each cracker a few times with a fork.

5   Bake for 15–20 minutes, until golden and crisp. Cool and break into squares.

Makes about 8 dozen 1½-inch crackers.

FLAX WHEAT THINS
Add 2 Tbsp ground flax seeds to the flour mixture, or sprinkle on top along with the salt.

TOMATO-BASIL WHEAT THINS
Use tomato or V-8 juice in place of the water, and add 1 tsp dried basil to the flour.

Savory Parmesan Biscotti

Just like you can add chocolate, nuts, or dried fruit to a basic cookie, you can add all sorts of salty, savory ingredients to these basic biscotti.

2 cups all-purpose flour

1½ tsp baking powder

½ tsp freshly ground black pepper

¼ tsp salt

¼ cup butter, chilled

2 tsp chopped fresh rosemary (optional)

½ cup grated Parmesan cheese

½ cup milk

2 large eggs

½ cup chopped dried figs, black olives, or sun-dried tomatoes (optional)

lightly beaten egg white (optional)

Per biscotti:

Calories	97
Total fat	4.2 g
saturated fat	2.4 g
monounsaturated fat	1.2 g
polyunsaturated fat	0.2 g
Protein	3.5 g
Carbohydrates	11.1 g
Cholesterol	33.3 mg
Fiber	0.4 g
Calories from fat	39%

1   Preheat oven to 350°F.

2   In a large bowl or in the bowl of a food processor, combine the flour, baking powder, pepper, and salt. Add the butter and rosemary (if using) and blend in with a fork or your fingertips, or pulse the food processor until they're incorporated. (Alternatively, melt the butter in a small saucepan and continue to cook for about 5 minutes or until it turns a nutty brown, then add it, along with the rosemary if using, to the dry ingredients.) Stir in the Parmesan cheese.

3   In a small bowl, whisk together the milk and eggs. Add to the flour mixture and stir just until the dough begins to come together. If you like, add figs, olives, or tomatoes and mix (you may have to use your hands) until the dough is well blended.

4   On a baking sheet that has been sprayed with nonstick spray, shape the dough into a log about 2 inches wide and ¾ inch thick. If you like, brush the tops with a little beaten egg white to give it a shiny finish. (It could really be shaped into any length you like—make it wider or narrower for longer or shorter biscotti.)

5   Bake for 25–30 minutes, until firm and starting to crack on top. Cool the log on a wire rack and reduce oven temperature to 275°F.

6 Place the cooled log on a cutting board and cut into ½-inch-thick slices with a sharp, serrated knife. Place the biscotti upright on the baking sheet and bake for another 30 minutes, until slightly golden and firm. Cool on the pan or transfer to a wire rack. If you like your biscotti particularly hard, turn the oven off, but leave them inside to cool.

Makes about 1½ dozen biscotti.

Roasted Garlic Potato Skins

I realize these don't exactly fit into the "cracker" category, but they are crispy and make great, sturdy scoopers for any kind of dip. Most of a potato's nutrients are in or just underneath the skin, so this is a good way to eat them. (The baked potato chips on page 4 make great dippers too, especially when you slice unpeeled potatoes lengthwise, for deeper scoopability.)

4 medium russet (baking) potatoes

1 head garlic

1–2 Tbsp canola or olive oil

salt and pepper to taste

Per potato skin:

Calories	38
Total fat	0.9 g
saturated fat	0.1 g
monounsaturated fat	0.6 g
polyunsaturated fat	0.1 g
Protein	1 g
Carbohydrates	6.9 g
Cholesterol	0 mg
Fiber	0.6 g
Calories from fat	20%

1   Preheat oven to 350°F.

2   Scrub each potato and poke it once or twice with a fork. Cut a thin slice off the top of the head of garlic and wrap it in foil. Bake the garlic and potatoes for about an hour, until the potatoes are tender. Remove from the oven and set the potatoes on a rack until they are cool enough to handle. Open the foil and let the garlic cool. Turn the oven up to 450°F. (If you're doing this in advance, everything can be baked up to this point and then refrigerated for 24 hours, until you're ready for them.)

3   Quarter the potatoes lengthwise and scoop out the flesh (keep it for another use—it makes great home fries the next day), leaving ¼-inch-thick skins. Spread them out, skin side down, on a baking sheet.

4   Squeeze the roasted garlic into a small bowl and mash it into a paste with the oil and salt and pepper, using a fork. Spread the garlic paste generously onto the potato skins.

5   Bake for 20–25 minutes, until golden.

Makes 16 potato skins.

CHILI, CHEESE & GARLIC SKINS
Sprinkle each potato skin with a mixture of ¼ cup grated Parmesan cheese and 1 tsp chili powder after spreading them with the garlic paste.

Bagel Chips

This is a great way to resurrect stale bagels. Plain bagel chips make perfect scoops for thick dips and spreads, but if you want them to have flavor on their own, use onion or garlic bagels to begin with or toss them with a bit of oil and any seasonings you like before you bake them.

bagels, any flavor

any seasonings you choose: coarse salt, sesame seeds, Parmesan cheese, herbs, or powdered ranch dressing mix

Per chip (plain):

Calories	10
Total fat	0 g
saturated fat	0 g
monounsaturated fat	0 g
polyunsaturated fat	0 g
Protein	0.4 g
Carbohydrates	2.1 g
Cholesterol	1 mg
Fiber	0 g
Calories from fat	9%

1 Preheat oven to 350°F.

2 Slice bagels into thin round slices and, if you like, toss in a plastic bag with the seasonings of your choice. (They should be moist enough for the flavors to adhere; if not, spray them lightly with non-stick spray or toss with a bit of canola or olive oil.) Spread out in a single layer on a baking sheet and bake for 5–7 minutes, until golden.

Makes as many chips as you like.

OLIVE OIL & GARLIC BAGEL CHIPS

Stir a clove of crushed garlic into 1 Tbsp olive oil and toss the chips in it to coat well before baking. (A tablespoon is enough for 2 bagels.)

Pita Chips

If you want to cut back on fat even further, omit the oil and spray the pitas lightly with nonstick spray to help the seasonings adhere, or bake them absolutely plain. If you're cooking outdoors you could do them on the grill; brush whole, split pitas with oil and grill on the barbecue until grill-marked and crisp, then break into wedges.

3 pita bread rounds, white or whole wheat

olive or canola oil, for brushing (optional)

1 clove garlic, crushed (optional)

any additions you like: onion or garlic powder, freshly ground black pepper, lemon pepper, basil, dried Italian seasoning, grated Parmesan cheese, 5-spice powder, or any other herb or spice of your choice

Per chip (plain using 1 Tbsp olive oil):

Calories	13
Total fat	0.2 g
saturated fat	0 g
monounsaturated fat	0.2 g
polyunsaturated fat	0 g
Protein	0.3 g
Carbohydrates	2.1 g
Cholesterol	0 mg
Fiber	0.1 g
Calories from fat	22%

1 Preheat oven to 375°F.

2 Cut pitas in half and then split them around the edge. Stir the garlic into a small ramekin of oil and brush the rough side of the pitas lightly with it. Stack them and cut into wedges with a knife.

3 Place pita wedges in a single layer on a baking sheet and sprinkle with your choice of flavorings. (They are just as good left plain.)

4 Bake for 7–10 minutes, until golden and crisp. Store extras in a tightly sealed container.

Makes 2 dozen chips.

CURRIED PITA CHIPS
Mix ½ tsp curry powder or paste, ¼ tsp ground cumin, and a pinch of cayenne pepper into the oil and omit the garlic.

Crostini

Literally "little toasts" in Italian, crostini are toasted slices of baguette, often brushed with oil and/or rubbed with a cut clove of garlic. Cut the baguette on a slight diagonal so that the slices are easier to bite into. These little toasts can act as a vehicle for all sorts of toppings or be served alongside spreads or dips. The Parmesan crostini below are perfect with wine and a dish of good olives to nibble before dinner.

1 baguette, white, sourdough, or whole wheat

¼ cup olive or canola oil

1 large garlic clove, cut in half lengthwise

Per crostini:

Calories	37
Total fat	1.4 g
saturated fat	0.2 g
monounsaturated fat	1 g
polyunsaturated fat	0.2 g
Protein	0.9 g
Carbohydrates	5.2 g
Cholesterol	0 mg
Fiber	0.3 g
Calories from fat	34%

1   Preheat oven to 350°F.

2   Slice the baguette on a slight diagonal into slices about ½ inch thick. Place them in a single layer on a baking sheet and brush them lightly with olive oil. Toast for about 10 minutes, until pale golden around the edges. Rub the toasts with the cut side of the garlic clove while they're still warm.

Makes about 4 dozen crostini, depending on the size of your baguette.

ROSEMARY-PARMESAN CROSTINI
Stir together ½ cup grated Parmesan cheese, 2 Tbsp milk, 1 tsp chopped fresh rosemary, and a pinch of cayenne pepper; spread on the toasts (instead of brushing them with oil and rubbing with garlic) before baking.

Flour Tortillas

Homemade tortillas are far easier than they sound to make. They are also cheap and far superior to the store-bought kind. If you prefer whole wheat tortillas, use half or all whole wheat flour.

2 cups flour, all-purpose or whole wheat

½ tsp baking powder

¼ tsp salt

2 Tbsp canola or olive oil

⅔–¾ cup warm water

Per tortilla:

Calories	144
Total fat	3.7 g
saturated fat	0.3 g
monounsaturated fat	2 g
polyunsaturated fat	1.1 g
Protein	3.2 g
Carbohydrates	23.8 g
Cholesterol	0 mg
Fiber	1 g
Calories from fat	24%

1. In a large mixing bowl combine the flour, baking powder, and salt. Stir in the oil and half the water; continue to stir and add water until the dough comes together but is not too sticky. Knead on a lightly floured surface for about 5 minutes, until the dough is smooth and elastic.

2. If you have time at this point, cover the dough and let it sit at room temperature for half an hour (or up to several hours) to let the gluten relax.

3. Divide the dough into 8 balls. On a lightly floured surface, press each ball into a disc and then roll it out as thin as possible—it should be about 7–8 inches in diameter.

4. Cook the tortillas one at a time in a dry frying pan set over medium heat, until it blisters and brown spots begin to appear. It should take about a minute per side. Serve warm and store extras tightly wrapped.

Makes 8 tortillas.

MINI FLOUR TORTILLAS
Pinch off ¾-inch balls of dough and press with the back of a spatula to flatten. Bake several at a time as directed. Serve with dips or spreads, or fill and secure with a toothpick to make mini wraps.

Wonton Crisps

Wontons make crispy, low-fat chips and are sturdy enough to scoop up loads of dip. They're cheap too—one package of wonton wrappers typically costs under $2 and makes about 14 dozen crisps! All you need to do is cut the wontons in half—either into strips or triangles—and bake them until golden with your choice of seasoning.

fresh wonton wrappers (however many you want)

nonstick cooking spray (check that the ingredients are only oil) or canola or olive oil

Sesame, Garlic & Parmesan

1 Tbsp sesame seeds (optional)

1 Tbsp grated Parmesan cheese

1 tsp salt

½ tsp garlic powder

Cinnamon Sugar

1 Tbsp sugar

¼ tsp ground cinnamon

Spicy Curry

2 tsp curry powder

½ tsp salt

¼ tsp each cumin, chili powder, paprika, and garlic powder

pinch freshly ground black pepper

Salt & Pepper

½ tsp each salt and freshly ground black pepper

1 Preheat oven to 350°F.

2 Combine seasoning ingredients in a small bowl.

3 Cut stack of wontons diagonally into triangles or across into strips, then separate them and lay out in a single layer on a baking sheet. Lightly spray them with nonstick spray or brush them lightly with canola or olive oil. Sprinkle with your choice of seasoning mixture.

4 Bake for 5 minutes or until deep golden and crisp. Watch carefully—they darken quickly!

Makes as many crisps as you like.

Per crisp (plain):

Calories	12
Total fat	0 g
Saturated fat	0 g
monounsaturated fat	0 g
polyunsaturated fat	0 g
Protein	0.4 g
Carbohydrates	2.3 g
Cholesterol	0.4 mg
Fiber	0 g
Calories from fat	8%

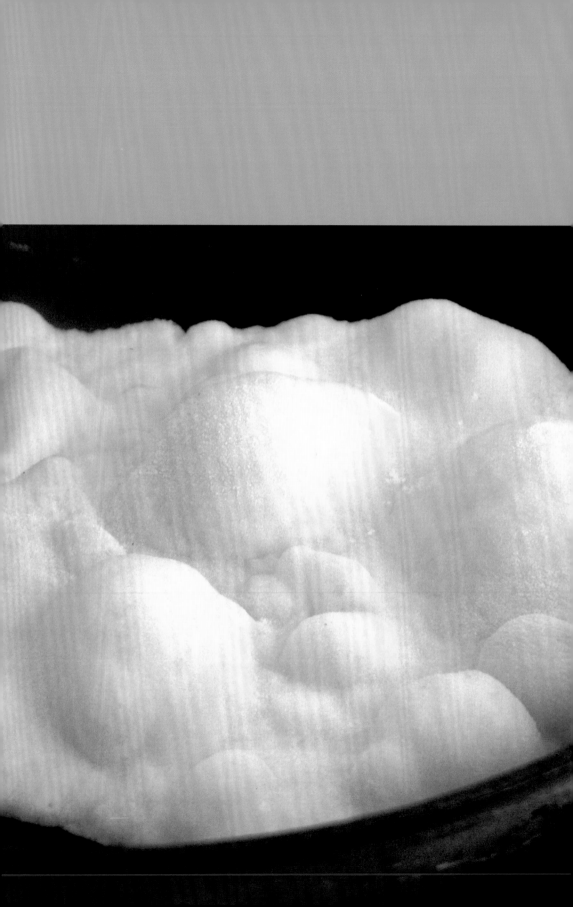

Naan

Chewy, bulbous naan—an Indian flatbread—has a slightly sour tang from the yogurt and makes wonderful dipping bread, particularly with Curried Daal Dip (page 71) or Hummus (page 68). Serve naan whole and tear off chunks as you need them, or cut them into strips. Day-old naan can be cut into wedges and toasted, much like pitas or tortillas. They also make a great base for pizza or a vehicle for wraps.

½ cup warm water

2½ tsp active dry yeast

1 tsp sugar

2½ cups all-purpose flour, plus extra for rolling

½ tsp salt

¼ cup canola oil

1 large egg, beaten

¼ cup plain yogurt

oil or melted butter, for cooking

Per naan:

Calories	177
Total fat	6.4 g
saturated fat	0.7 g
monounsaturated fat	3.5 g
polyunsaturated fat	1.8 g
Protein	4.5 g
Carbohydrates	25 g
Cholesterol	22 mg
Fiber	1.2 g
Calories from fat	33%

1 In a large bowl, stir together the water, yeast, and sugar and let stand for 5 minutes, until foamy. If it doesn't foam, the yeast is inactive; toss it out!

2 Stir in the flour, salt, canola oil, and egg, and stir until almost combined. Add the yogurt and work into a soft, pliable dough. Cover with a tea towel and let rise for an hour or two, until doubled in size.

3 Divide the dough into 6–8 pieces and on a lightly floured surface, roll out each piece into an oval. Lightly brush both sides with oil or melted butter. Cook each naan in a hot frying pan set over high heat until blistered and cooked, flipping with tongs as necessary.

Makes about 10 naan breads.

Easy Breadsticks

These crunchy nibbles are quick to make and can be flavored with almost anything. They are as fitting for a party as they are for kids' snacks; serve them in a tall glass or vase alongside a cheese platter, or tuck them into lunch boxes. They can be dressed up or dressed down, depending on the occasion; try any of the suggested flavorings or a combination of them, or experiment with your own additions.

1 cup all-purpose flour

1 cup whole wheat flour

1 tsp baking powder

½ tsp salt

any additions you like: ¼ cup Parmesan cheese, 2 Tbsp fresh rosemary, 1 Tbsp pesto, ¼ cup sun-dried tomatoes (use their oil in place of the oil below), ¼ cup pitted black olives, ½ cup grated sharp cheese, ¼ cup crumbled blue cheese, ¼–½ cup finely chopped nuts, 1 crushed garlic clove

3 Tbsp canola or olive oil

½–¾ cup cold water or milk

coarse salt, for sprinkling (optional)

Per stick (plain):

Calories	51
Total fat	1.8 g
saturated fat	0.3 g
monounsaturated fat	1.3 g
polyunsaturated fat	0.2 g
Protein	1.2 g
Carbohydrates	7.7 g
Cholesterol	0 mg
Fiber	0.8 g
Calories from fat	31%

1 Preheat oven to 400°F.

2 Combine the flours, baking powder, and salt in the bowl of a food processor and pulse to combine. Add any flavorings you like and pulse until chopped and blended with the flour mixture. Add the oil and pulse until the mixture resembles coarse meal. (Alternatively, blend everything together in a bowl with a spatula or whisk.)

3 With the machine running, pour ½ cup of cold water or milk through the feed tube and pulse, adding extra if you need it until the dough starts to come together. This will depend on your flour and what flavorings you added; I usually need ½ cup plus about 2 Tbsp of liquid.

4 Tip the dough out onto a lightly floured surface, gather it into a ball, and let it rest for about 10 minutes. Roll the dough out about ¼ inch thick, sprinkle it with salt (if you like), and roll lightly to help the salt adhere. Cut into ¼-inch- to ½-inch-wide strips as long or short as you like, then twist the strips and place them on an ungreased baking sheet, pressing the ends lightly onto the sheet if they start to unravel. Bake for 12–15 minutes, or until golden.

Makes about 2 dozen breadsticks.

Dip, Spread, Dunk & Smear

There's something indulgent about dipping one food into another. I confess I am more a scooper than a dipper, the goal for me being to get as much dip onto my cracker or veg as it can structurally tolerate.

People think dips are just for parties, but reusable containers make dips just as portable as any other snack. Hummus is one of my favorites to eat at my desk or take on road trips with torn-up pitas and fresh veggies. Mix up a dip instead of popcorn when you're watching a movie, or put some out on the table when the kids are doing their homework or everyone comes to play Scrabble. Dip makes a great motivational tool to get vegetable haters to eat their veggies, but try dunking fruit, flatbread, breadsticks, baked tortilla chips, potato skins, and crackers too. Most dips keep very well in the fridge, so don't be afraid to make a big batch.

Baked Spinach & Artichoke Dip

If you don't like your dip chunky, put everything in the food processor and pulse it until it's as smooth as you like. If you want to prep it ahead for a party, you can keep it finished in the fridge until it's time to pop in the oven.

one 14 oz can artichoke hearts, drained and finely chopped

1 pkg frozen chopped spinach, thawed

½ cup light sour cream or plain yogurt

half an 8 oz pkg light cream cheese (not fat free)

¼ cup light mayonnaise

¼ cup grated Parmesan or Romano cheese

1 garlic clove, finely chopped

salt and pepper to taste

½ cup grated part-skim mozzarella and/or an extra 2–4 Tbsp grated Parmesan

Per serving:

Calories	125
Total fat	7.1 g
saturated fat	3.1 g
monounsaturated fat	2.6 g
polyunsaturated fat	0.8 g
Protein	6.9 g
Carbohydrates	10.2 g
Cholesterol	15.9 mg
Fiber	3.2 g
Calories from fat	48%

1 Preheat oven to 375°F.

2 Finely chop or pulse the artichoke hearts and spinach with the sour cream or yogurt in a food processor until roughly chopped. In a bowl, mash together the cream cheese, mayo, Parmesan cheese, garlic, and salt and pepper until well blended. Stir in the artichoke-spinach mixture and spread in a shallow baking dish. Sprinkle with grated mozzarella or more Parmesan cheese.

3 Bake until heated through and bubbly, about 25 minutes. Serve warm with tortilla chips or sliced soft, crusty baguette.

Serves 8.

Hot Crab & Artichoke Dip

There's no reason in the world that you should stop eating gooey crab dip packed with cheese; just make sure you don't polish off the whole thing yourself. Omit the artichokes if you want just a plain old cheesy crab dip, or replace it with half a package of frozen spinach, thawed, with the extra moisture squeezed out. If it seems too thick for your taste, thin it with a little milk.

one 8 oz tub light cream cheese

1 cup low-fat sour cream

2 Tbsp lemon juice

2 Tbsp grated purple onion

1 tsp Worcestershire sauce

1 garlic clove, crushed

2–3 dashes hot pepper sauce (optional)

½ tsp dry mustard

salt and pepper to taste

½–1 lb crabmeat, cartilage removed (or two 6 oz cans, drained)

one 14 oz can artichoke hearts, drained and chopped

½ cup grated old cheddar cheese

1 Preheat oven to 350°F.

2 In a large bowl, beat the cream cheese until smooth. Stir in sour cream, lemon juice, onion, Worcestershire sauce, garlic, hot sauce, mustard, and salt and pepper. Stir in the crabmeat, artichoke hearts, and cheese.

3 Spoon into a shallow baking dish or pie plate and bake for 20–30 minutes, until heated through and bubbly around the edges. Serve warm with baked tortillas, crackers, pita, bagel chips, or fresh veggies.

Serves 8.

Per serving:

Calories	165
Total fat	8.6 g
saturated fat	4.8 g
monounsaturated fat	2.5 g
polyunsaturated fat	0.5 g
Protein	12.3 g
Carbohydrates	10.2 g
Cholesterol	41.4 mg
Fiber	2.3 g
Calories from fat	46%

Curried Shrimp Chutney Dip

I have not met anyone (without a seafood allergy) who doesn't love this dip, and it takes about 5 minutes to stir together. It's one of those recipes that produces spectacular results with minimal effort. It's equally delicious made with crab, or try a combination of shrimp and crab.

half an 8 oz tub light cream cheese

½ cup light sour cream

2 green onions, finely chopped

1 roasted red pepper (page 78), finely chopped

⅓ cup mango or peach chutney

1 garlic clove, crushed

1 tsp curry powder or paste, or to taste

salt and pepper to taste

1 lb cooked shrimp, chopped, or small cocktail shrimp

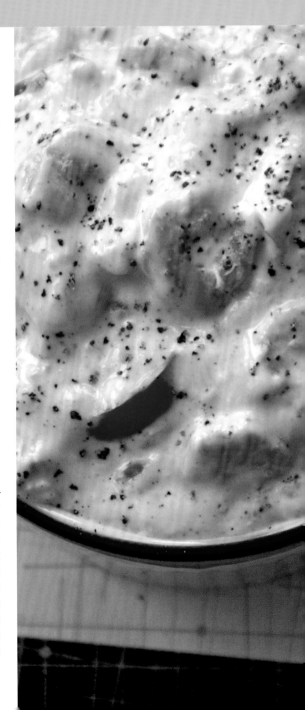

1 Combine the cream cheese and sour cream in a medium bowl and beat until smooth. Stir in the remaining ingredients except the shrimp, and stir until smooth. Stir in the shrimp.

2 Transfer to a serving bowl and refrigerate for at least an hour or overnight. Serve with fresh naan, veggies, or pita.

Serves 10.

Per serving:

Calories	117
Total fat	3.6 g
saturated fat	1.8 g
monounsaturated fat	1 g
polyunsaturated fat	0.4 g
Protein	11.2 g
Carbohydrates	10 g
Cholesterol	78 mg
Fiber	0.4 g
Calories from fat	28%

Caramelized Onion Dip

If you want to do this right—and you might as well if you're going to indulge—try homemade potato chips (page 4) with this dip. Dips made with those packets of French onion soup are loaded with salt and additives—this recipe is much healthier (and tastier too!). Sometimes I add a few tablespoons of beef stock to the onions while they are caramelizing to add flavor.

1 Tbsp canola or olive oil

3 large sweet onions (such as Vidalia or Walla Walla) or yellow onions, peeled, halved, and thinly sliced

2 garlic cloves, crushed

1 Tbsp balsamic vinegar

1 cup low-fat or light sour cream

salt and pepper to taste

Per ¼ cup:

Calories	81
Total fat	4.1 g
saturated fat	1.4 g
monounsaturated fat	1.9 g
polyunsaturated fat	0.8 g
Protein	2.6 g
Carbohydrates	8 g
Cholesterol	6.7 mg
Fiber	0.6 g
Calories from fat	47%

1   In a large frying pan, heat the oil over medium heat; add the onions and cook, stirring often, for about 10 minutes or until golden and caramelized. Add the garlic and balsamic vinegar and cook for another 2 minutes, until deep golden. Set aside to cool slightly.

2   Transfer to a medium bowl and stir in the sour cream and salt and pepper. If you want it more finely chopped or smooth, pulse it in the food processor. Cover and chill for at least an hour before serving.

Makes about 1½ cups.

Chili Con Queso Dip

I am a huge cheese fan. I love all kinds of cheese, except the low-fat kind, which tends to have a rubbery texture and hardly any flavor—you end up using twice as much in an attempt to satisfy yourself. I much prefer sharp cheeses such as old cheddar, which is intensely flavored, so a little goes a long way. Add a small can of chopped green chilies if you want to spice this up.

1 tsp canola or olive oil

1 small onion, chopped

2 garlic cloves, crushed

1 Tbsp flour

one 14 oz can diced tomatoes, undrained

1 cup salsa

½–1 tsp chili powder

salt and pepper to taste

half an 8 oz pkg light cream cheese, cubed

1 cup grated old cheddar cheese

1. In a large skillet, heat the oil over medium heat and sauté the onions and garlic until soft. Add the flour and cook for another minute—the mixture will be dry. Add the diced tomatoes, salsa, chili powder, and salt and pepper and bring to a simmer.

2. Reduce heat to low and add the cream cheese. Stir until it's almost melted, then add the grated cheddar and stir until all the cheese is melted and smooth.

3. Serve warm with baked tortilla chips.

   Serves 8.

SPINACH CON QUESO DIP
Add one 1 lb package frozen chopped spinach, thawed and squeezed dry, to the onion and garlic mixture and sauté until the moisture has evaporated before adding the flour.

BEAN CON QUESO DIP
Stir a 14 oz can of refried beans (or mashed drained kidney beans) into the dip, and use a full 8 oz package of cream cheese.

Per serving:

Calories	101
Total fat	5.9 g
saturated fat	3.1 g
monounsaturated fat	2 g
polyunsaturated fat	0.5 g
Protein	4.3 g
Carbohydrates	8.4 g
Cholesterol	16 mg
Fiber	1.6 g
Calories from fat	51%

Seven-Layer Dip

This Seven-Layer Dip has closer to nine layers, but who's counting? If you don't want to bother with the bean layer, substitute a can of refried beans or vegetarian chili, which are usually much lower in fat than the meaty varieties. Some people like this hot and bubbly—if this sounds like you, omit the lettuce and bake it at 350°F for about 20 minutes, until it's heated through.

Bean layer

one 14 oz can kidney beans, rinsed and drained

1 garlic clove, crushed

1 Tbsp lime juice

½ tsp chili powder

½ tsp cumin

pinch salt

1 Tbsp taco seasoning (optional)

1 cup low-fat sour cream

2 ripe tomatoes, diced

½ cup salsa

1 small red, green, or yellow bell pepper, seeded and diced

1 ripe avocado, peeled, pitted, and mashed, or 1 batch Guacamole (page 61)

1 small purple onion, finely chopped

2 cups shredded iceberg lettuce

1 cup grated old cheddar cheese

¼ cup sliced black olives

1 Mash the beans with garlic, lime juice, chili powder, cumin, and salt in a food processor or in a bowl with a fork; spread in a shallow dish or pie plate. Stir the taco seasoning into the sour cream. Layer the remaining ingredients, except the tortilla chips, on top of the beans in any order you like.

2 Serve immediately with baked tortilla chips, or cover and chill until you're ready for it.

Serves 10.

Per serving:

Calories	144
Total fat	6.9 g
saturated fat	2.5 g
monounsaturated fat	3.2 g
polyunsaturated fat	0.8 g
Protein	6.1 g
Carbohydrates	15.7 g
Cholesterol	9.8 mg
Fiber	1.7 g
Calories from fat	42%

Cheesy Black Bean Dip

Legumes are quite possibly the world's most perfect food; pound for pound they contain as much protein as beef, they are rich in soluble fiber (the best kind—and only 2 tablespoons of kidney beans gives you four times as much as one slice of whole wheat bread), and they are an excellent source of folic acid, calcium, iron, copper, phosphorus, potassium, magnesium, and zinc. And, of course, beans are low in fat and calories.

one 14 oz can black beans, rinsed and drained

1 tsp canola oil

1 small onion, finely chopped

2 garlic cloves, crushed

1 large tomato, chopped

½ cup salsa

1 Tbsp chili powder

½ tsp cumin

1 cup shredded old cheddar or Monterey Jack cheese

1 Tbsp lime juice

¼ cup chopped fresh cilantro

1   Mash the beans with a fork until chunky.

2   Heat the oil in a skillet over medium heat and sauté the onion and garlic for 3 minutes, until soft. Add the beans, tomato, salsa, chili powder, and cumin; cook for 5 more minutes, stirring often. Remove from heat and stir in the cheese; stir until the cheese melts, then stir in the lime juice and cilantro and remove from the heat.

3   Serve warm or at room temperature with tortilla chips.

Serves 8.

BLACK BEAN & BACON DIP
Cook 3 slices of bacon in the frying pan until crisp; crumble and set aside. Drain all but a tablespoon of the fat from the pan and sauté the onion and garlic in it instead of using the oil. Stir the crumbled bacon back into the dip along with the cheese.

Per serving:

Calories	123
Total fat	3.5 g
saturated fat	1.6 g
monounsaturated fat	1.1 g
polyunsaturated fat	0.4 g
Protein	7 g
Carbohydrates	17 g
Cholesterol	7.2 mg
Fiber	4.6 g
Calories from fat	25%

Chorizo-Chipotle Dip

If you can find chicken chorizo sausage, it has about a quarter the fat of regular chorizo sausage. But any Italian sausage will work just as well. (The nutritional analysis is based on regular uncooked chorizo.)

1 spicy chorizo sausage

canola or olive oil, for cooking (optional)

1 onion, finely chopped

1 red bell pepper, cored, seeded, and chopped

1–2 garlic cloves, crushed

½ tsp cumin

½ tsp oregano

one 19 oz can kidney, pinto, or navy beans, undrained

1 canned chipotle chile en adobo, finely chopped

½ cup low-fat sour cream

salt to taste

chopped fresh cilantro (optional)

Per serving:

Calories	148
Total fat	3.3 g
saturated fat	1.4 g
monounsaturated fat	0.8 g
polyunsaturated fat	0.9 g
Protein	9.4 g
Carbohydrates	21.2 g
Cholesterol	10 mg
Fiber	5.2 g
Calories from fat	19%

1 Squeeze the chorizo sausage out of its casing into a large frying pan (drizzled with a bit of oil, if you think it needs it) set over medium heat and cook, crumbling it up until no longer pink. Transfer to a small bowl.

2 If there is too much fat in the pan, drain most of it off and add a bit of canola or olive oil if you need to. Sauté the onion for 5 minutes, until soft; add the pepper and garlic and cook for a few more minutes. Add the cumin, oregano, beans, and chipotle pepper. Bring to a simmer, then reduce the heat and cook for about 10 minutes, stirring often.

3 Transfer the bean mixture to a food processor and pulse until it's chunky. Stir in the sausage, sour cream, and salt to taste.

4 Transfer to a serving bowl and top with fresh cilantro if you like.

Serves 8.

Guacamole

A simple guacamole is nothing more than avocados mashed with garlic and lime. Because avocados are very high in fat—about 75% of their calories come from fat—guacamole is fairly high in calories as well. But take heart, it's virtually all healthy monounsaturated fat, the kind you want to include in your diet. The only tricky part about guacamole is your avocados must be ripe or they won't mash very well. The best way to tell if an avocado is ripe is by squeezing it—a ripe avocado will yield to gentle pressure. If you need to ripen them fast, put them in a paper bag with an apple.

2 ripe avocados, peeled and pitted

1 garlic clove, crushed

juice of 1 lime

salt to taste

¼ tsp ground cumin (optional)

2 Tbsp finely chopped or grated purple onion (optional)

2 Tbsp chopped fresh cilantro (optional)

a few chopped cherry or grape tomatoes (optional)

Per serving:

Calories	111
Total fat	10.3 g
saturated fat	1.6 g
monounsaturated fat	6.4 g
polyunsaturated fat	1.3 g
Protein	1.4 g
Carbohydrates	5.8 g
Cholesterol	0 mg
Fiber	1.8 g
Calories from fat	76%

1   Mash everything (except the tomatoes, if you're using them) together with a fork to make it as smooth or as chunky as you like. Stir in the tomatoes if you're using them.

Serves 6.

GUACAMOLE WITH GRAPES OR POMEGRANATE
Add a handful of halved purple grapes or pomegranate seeds to the finished guacamole instead of the tomatoes.

Guacamole lends itself well to all kinds of additions—also try stirring in ½ cup salsa or sour cream, a head of roasted garlic, or a handful of chopped cooked shrimp.

Classic Tomato Salsa

Salsa has hardly any calories and is packed with nutrients and antioxidants (especially carotenoids like beta-carotene and lycopene). Try roasting the tomatoes first under the broiler until they're blackened to add a smoky flavor.

3 ripe tomatoes, finely chopped

1 garlic clove, crushed

3 Tbsp finely chopped purple onion

1 Tbsp lime juice

1 jalapeño pepper, seeded and minced (or more if you like it hot!)

2 Tbsp chopped fresh cilantro or basil

salt to taste

1   Stir everything together in a bowl.

    Makes about 2½ cups.

Per ½ cup:

Calories	21
Total fat	0.3 g
saturated fat	0 g
monounsaturated fat	0 g
polyunsaturated fat	0.1 g
Protein	0.8 g
Carbohydrates	4.7 g
Cholesterol	0 mg
Fiber	1 g
Calories from fat	11%

AVOCADO SALSA

Stir a chopped ripe avocado into the salsa.

Black Bean & Mango Salsa

Sweet, juicy mango is rich in vitamins A and C and makes a delicious contrast to protein-packed black beans.

1 ripe mango

one 19 oz can black beans, rinsed and drained

¼ cup finely chopped red onion

2 Tbsp chopped fresh cilantro

1 finely chopped jalapeño pepper and/or canned chipotle chile in adobo sauce

a few drops Tabasco sauce

salt to taste

1   Dice the mango by slicing it lengthwise along the flat stone to remove both "cheeks." Score them without cutting through the skin, then flip them inside out and cut the flesh off the skin.

2   Stir everything together in a bowl.

    Makes about 2½ cups.

Per ½ cup:

Calories	174
Total fat	0.7 g
saturated fat	0.2 g
monounsaturated fat	0.1 g
polyunsaturated fat	0.3 g
Protein	9.9 g
Carbohydrates	33.7 g
Cholesterol	0 mg
Fiber	8.5 g
Calories from fat	4%

Olive, Feta & Basil Salsa

This is a different and intensely flavored salsa; try it stuffed into mini pitas with grilled chicken or hummus.

4 ripe tomatoes, finely chopped

¼ cup crumbled feta

¼–½ cup fresh basil, torn or chopped

¼ cup sliced pitted kalamata olives

1 Tbsp capers

1 Tbsp olive oil

pinch sugar

salt and freshly ground pepper to taste

1   Stir everything together in a bowl.

    Makes about 3 cups.

Per ½ cup:

Calories	46
Total fat	3.3 g
saturated fat	0.5 g
monounsaturated fat	2.3 g
polyunsaturated fat	0.4 g
Protein	0.8 g
Carbohydrates	4.2 g
Cholesterol	0 mg
Fiber	1.3 g
Calories from fat	60%

Pico de Gallo

Some times of the year it's hard to find nice tomatoes at the market, but it's always easy to get your hands on a can of them. Use a large (28 oz) good-quality can such as Muir Glen fire-roasted tomatoes instead of fresh tomatoes if you want.

3 ripe tomatoes, finely chopped

one 14 oz can diced tomatoes, drained

½ purple or sweet, mild onion, finely chopped

2 fresh jalapeño peppers, seeded and minced, or more to taste

½ bunch fresh cilantro

juice of 1 lime (or 2 Tbsp)

2 garlic cloves, crushed

1 Tbsp sugar

1 Tbsp olive oil

½ tsp ground cumin

½ tsp salt

1   Stir everything together in a large bowl, crushing the tomatoes if they are too chunky. Drain off some of the juice if it is too watery. If you want to use a food processor, pulse the onion, garlic, and peppers first until finely chopped. Add everything else and pulse once or twice, until blended but still chunky.

Makes about 3 cups.

Per ½ cup:

Calories	65
Total fat	2.8 g
saturated fat	0.4 g
monounsaturated fat	1.7 g
polyunsaturated fat	0.4 g
Protein	1.6 g
Carbohydrates	10.2 g
Cholesterol	0 mg
Fiber	1.8 g
Calories from fat	35%

Peanut Sauce

Peanut sauce is a wonderful thing. Double the recipe if you want leftovers to pour over cold noodles or dip satay, lettuce wraps, rice-paper rolls, grilled chicken, or shrimp. Use more or less broth to make the sauce as thick or thin as you like. If you like coconut flavor in your peanut sauce but not the fat of coconut milk, add a teaspoon of coconut extract.

2–4 Tbsp chicken or vegetable broth or coconut milk

¼ cup all-natural or light peanut butter

3 Tbsp soy sauce

2 Tbsp brown sugar or honey

2 Tbsp rice vinegar or lime juice

1 garlic clove, crushed

1–2 tsp grated fresh ginger

1 tsp sesame oil (optional)

¼–½ tsp curry paste (optional)

1 Combine all the ingredients in a blender or jar and whiz or shake until smooth. Refrigerate until you're ready to serve it.

Makes about 1 cup.

Per tablespoon:

Calories	28
Total fat	1.4 g
saturated fat	0.3 g
monounsaturated fat	0.6 g
polyunsaturated fat	0.5 g
Protein	0.9 g
Carbohydrates	3.4 g
Cholesterol	0 mg
Fiber	0 g
Calories from fat	42%

Dukkah

Dukkah is a fantastic blend of spices and nuts that you could eat out of hand or sprinkle on salads, but its intended serving method is to put it out in a shallow bowl alongside crusty bread and good olive oil; you dip the bread into the oil and then into the dukkah. So since there is dipping action involved, here it is. If there is a snack out there that's good for your heart, this is it.

¾ cup hazelnuts or whole almonds

½ cup sesame seeds

2 Tbsp coriander seeds

2 Tbsp cumin seeds

1 tsp flaky sea salt

1 Tbsp freshly ground black pepper

Per tablespoon:

Calories	55
Total fat	5.1 g
saturated fat	0.5 g
monounsaturated fat	3 g
polyunsaturated fat	1.2 g
Protein	1.8 g
Carbohydrates	1.8 g
Cholesterol	0 mg
Fiber	0.7 g
Calories from fat	76%

1   Preheat the oven to 375°F.

2   Spread the hazelnuts out on a baking sheet and roast for 5–10 minutes, or until golden and fragrant. Transfer them onto a tea towel, fold the towel over, and rub them to remove as much of the skins as you can; set aside to cool. (If you're using almonds, toast them but don't worry about removing the skins.)

3   In a dry frying pan, toast the sesame seeds over medium heat, shaking the pan often, until golden and fragrant. Transfer to a bowl. Add the coriander and cumin seeds to the pan and toast until they begin to pop; transfer to a food processor with the hazelnuts and pulse until finely ground, then add to the sesame seeds and stir to combine them. Season with salt and pepper and blend well.

Makes about 1¼ cups.

Hummus

There are so many ways to make hummus, and it is one of the fastest snacks around. You can whiz up a batch in under five minutes in the food processor. I love eating it for lunch at my desk with a fresh pita to tear and dip, and it makes a great TV or movie snack instead of popcorn or chips. If you don't have tahini, peanut butter makes a delicious substitute. (And if you miss the sesame flavor tahini gives your hummus, a drizzle of sesame oil will do the trick.)

one 19 oz can chickpeas (garbanzo beans), rinsed and drained

2 Tbsp tahini (sesame seed paste) or peanut butter

2 Tbsp plain yogurt

2 garlic cloves, peeled

juice of 1 lemon (or 2–3 Tbsp)

½ tsp ground cumin (optional)

salt to taste

2–4 Tbsp olive oil

Per ¼ cup:

Calories	133
Total fat	5.6 g
saturated fat	0.7 g
monounsaturated fat	2.9 g
polyunsaturated fat	1.5 g
Protein	5.5 g
Carbohydrates	16.3 g
Cholesterol	0.2 mg
Fiber	2.8 g
Calories from fat	37%

1   Put the chickpeas, tahini, yogurt, garlic, lemon juice, cumin, and salt in the bowl of a food processor and pulse until puréed. With the motor running, drizzle in the olive oil until it's smooth and has the texture you want. If it's too thick, add a little extra oil, yogurt, or water.

2   Taste and adjust seasonings (salt and pepper, lemon juice, tahini) to your taste. Serve with fresh or toasted pita chips and/or fresh vegetables.

Makes about 2½ cups.

ROASTED RED PEPPER HUMMUS
Whiz in 2 roasted red peppers (page 78) and include the cumin.

CHIPOTLE–RED PEPPER HUMMUS
Whiz in 2 roasted red peppers (page 78) and a canned chipotle en adobo.

MEDITERRANEAN HUMMUS
Once the hummus is blended and smooth, stir in ¼–½ cup chopped kalamata olives, ¼–½ cup crumbled feta, and a small jar of artichoke hearts, drained and finely chopped.

ROASTED GARLIC HUMMUS
Substitute a head of roasted garlic, the cloves squeezed out of their papers, for the fresh garlic. (To roast garlic, wrap it in foil and tuck in a 350°F–400°F oven for 45 minutes to an hour.)

BALSAMIC ONION HUMMUS

Sauté a large chopped onion in a drizzle of
canola or olive oil for about 10 minutes, or
until golden. Add 2 Tbsp balsamic vinegar
and cook until it evaporates; cool and pulse
into hummus, leaving it slightly chunky.

PUMPKIN HUMMUS

Add a big spoonful—or up to a cup—of
canned pumpkin purée, and include the
cumin. (This is a great use of leftover
pumpkin.)

SPICED HUMMUS

Add 1 tsp chili powder, 1 tsp paprika, ½ tsp
curry powder or paste, ½ tsp cumin, and a
pinch of red pepper flakes.

EDAMAME HUMMUS

Substitute 1½ cups cooked edamame (soybeans) or a can of soybeans for the chickpeas,
or add a cup to the chickpeas. Replace the
fresh garlic with a head of roasted garlic and
top with fresh cilantro.

ROASTED CARROT HUMMUS

Add 2–3 roasted carrots (to roast them, peel,
cut into chunks, toss with oil, and roast at
400°F for half an hour, or until tender), and
double the amount of tahini and cumin.

GREEN PEA HUMMUS

Add a cup or two of frozen or shelled green
peas, boiled until tender, and ¼ cup fresh
cilantro.

Curried Daal (Lentil) Dip

Daal is a preparation of pulses, such as lentils, that have been split; it often refers to a thick, spicy Indian or Pakistani stew as well. This reminds me of a sort of Indian spiced hummus; purée it in the food processor if you want a similar consistency, but I like it chunky. Serve with fresh naan or pita chips.

1 cup dried orange lentils

canola oil, for cooking

1 small onion, chopped

2 garlic cloves, crushed

2–3 tsp curry paste

½ cup tomato sauce

1 tsp sugar

1 tsp chili powder

½ tsp salt

½ cup plain yogurt, half & half, evaporated milk, or light coconut milk

1 tsp coconut extract (optional)

½ tsp garam masala (optional)

chopped fresh cilantro (optional)

Per ¼ cup:

Calories	78
Total fat	0.8 g
saturated fat	0.2 g
monounsaturated fat	0.3 g
polyunsaturated fat	0.2 g
Protein	5.5 g
Carbohydrates	13 g
Cholesterol	0.6 mg
Fiber	2.2 g
Calories from fat	9%

1   In a medium pot, cover the lentils with plenty of water and boil for 20 minutes, until very well done, even mushy. Drain them and set aside.

2   Meanwhile, heat about a teaspoon of oil in a frying pan set over medium-high heat and sauté the onions for 5 minutes, or until golden. Add the garlic and curry paste and cook for another minute. Add the tomato sauce, sugar, chili powder, and salt, then the lentils and cook for another 5 minutes. Add the yogurt or cream and cook until well blended and thick.

3   Remove from heat and stir in the coconut extract and garam masala, if using. If you want the dip perfectly smooth, purée it in the food processor. Transfer to a serving bowl and sprinkle with cilantro, if you like.

Makes about 3 cups.

Roasted Garlic & White Bean Spread

Beans make a great base for dips and spreads, so I've tried to come up with as many uses for them as possible. A small container of bean spread with a baggie of crackers and veggies makes a great portable snack or lunch at your desk.

1 large head garlic

one 19 oz can white kidney beans, rinsed and drained

1 Tbsp olive oil

1 Tbsp lemon juice

salt to taste

a few drops of Tabasco sauce (optional)

1 Tbsp chopped fresh rosemary or sage (optional)

Per ¼ cup:

Calories	99
Total fat	1.8 g
saturated fat	0.3 g
monounsaturated fat	1.1 g
polyunsaturated fat	0.3 g
Protein	5.6 g
Carbohydrates	15.9 g
Cholesterol	0 mg
Fiber	4.1 g
Calories from fat	16%

1 Preheat the oven to 350°F.

2 Cut a thin slice off the top of the head of garlic and wrap it in foil. Bake for about an hour, until the garlic is soft and golden. (You can do several heads at a time, or throw a head or two in the oven when you're baking something else. Store the roasted garlic in the fridge until you're ready for it.)

3 In the bowl of a food processor combine the beans, olive oil, lemon juice, and salt, and if you like, the Tabasco and rosemary or sage. Squeeze the roasted cloves of garlic out of their skins into the food processor and pulse a few times to combine the ingredients—process it completely if you want a smooth dip, or leave it chunky.

4 Serve with crostini, pita chips, breadsticks, crackers, or veggies.

Makes about 2¼ cups.

BAKED WHITE BEAN SPREAD
Sauté a chopped onion in a drizzle of canola or olive oil until golden; stir into the finished dip. Spread in an ovenproof dish and sprinkle with grated Parmesan cheese or crumble over some goat cheese. Bake at 350°F for 20–30 minutes, until bubbly around the edges.

Tzatziki

Regular yogurt, preferably thick Greek yogurt, is far superior to the runny low-fat or fat-free varieties that are so commonly found at the grocery store. Even "full fat" yogurt generally contains only about 3 grams per half cup, and is much more delicious and satisfying.

WHITE BEAN & ROASTED PEPPER SPREAD

Add a roasted red pepper and ½ cup chopped fresh basil and process as directed.

ITALIAN WHITE BEAN SPREAD

Stir a small, finely chopped onion and a chopped roasted red pepper into the dip, along with about 1 Tbsp Italian dressing and ¼ cup chopped fresh parsley. Spread in an ovenproof dish and sprinkle with grated Parmesan cheese. Bake at 350°F for 20–30 minutes, until bubbly around the edges.

YOGURT & FETA WHITE BEAN SPREAD

Add 1 cup plain yogurt and ½ cup crumbled feta cheese and blend as directed. Stir in a chopped green onion, or sprinkle it overtop.

WHITE BEAN GUACAMOLE

Stir a mashed ripe avocado into the bean mixture, and use lime juice instead of lemon. At the end, stir in 1 chopped tomato and 2 Tbsp chopped fresh cilantro.

---

1 small English cucumber, unpeeled

1–2 garlic cloves, crushed

2 cups good-quality plain yogurt, preferably Balkan style

squeeze of lemon juice

salt and pepper to taste

---

1   Grate the cucumber with a box grater onto a double thickness of paper towel. Gather up the cucumber in the towel and squeeze out as much excess water as you can.

2   Combine the cucumber, garlic, yogurt, lemon juice, and salt and pepper in a bowl and stir until well blended. Chill for at least a couple hours or overnight; the garlic flavor will intensify as it sits.

Makes 2½–3 cups.

Per ⅓ cup:

Calories	45
Total fat	1 g
saturated fat	0.6 g
monounsaturated fat	0.3 g
polyunsaturated fat	0.1 g
Protein	3.5 g
Carbohydrates	5.6 g
Cholesterol	3.7 mg
Fiber	0.3 g
Calories from fat	20%

Muhammara

I am completely hooked on *muhammara*—a thick Middle Eastern dip made with walnuts, roasted red peppers, and tangy pomegranate molasses. You can get away with using less olive oil if you're concerned about calories, or more if you want a more robust dip. Pomegranate molasses can be found at Mediterranean grocery stores and is well worth the effort to find. It keeps well, so don't worry about using such a small amount.

3 red bell peppers, roasted (page 78)

½ cup walnuts, toasted

½ cup fresh breadcrumbs

2–4 garlic cloves, crushed

2 Tbsp pomegranate molasses

¼ tsp cumin (optional)

pinch red pepper flakes

2–6 Tbsp olive oil or walnut oil

Per ¼ cup:

Calories	180
Total fat	11 g
saturated fat	1.1 g
monounsaturated fat	4.8 g
polyunsaturated fat	4.5 g
Protein	4.5 g
Carbohydrates	18 g
Cholesterol	0 mg
Fiber	2.2 g
Calories from fat	52%

1   In the bowl of a food processor, pulse the roasted peppers, walnuts, breadcrumbs, garlic, pomegranate molasses, cumin (if you like), and red pepper flakes until well blended and smooth.

2   With the motor running, slowly pour the olive oil through the feed tube until the mixture is smooth and creamy. If it's too thick, add a few spoonfuls of water. To serve, spread the muhammara in a bowl, top with a walnut half, and drizzle with a little extra olive oil if you like. Serve with fresh pitas or pita chips.

Makes about 1½ cups.

Baba Ghanouj

Baba ghanouj (pronounced *ganoosh*) is a Middle Eastern dip made with roasted eggplant. It's perfect paired with hummus, roasted red pepper dip, and a big bowl of pita chips. Be warned—you will have garlic breath.

2 medium eggplants

¼ cup tahini (sesame seed paste)

2 garlic cloves, crushed

2 Tbsp lemon juice

1 tsp salt, or to taste

drizzle of olive oil

Per ⅓ cup:

Calories	66
Total fat	3.4 g
saturated fat	0.5 g
monounsaturated fat	1.2 g
polyunsaturated fat	1.5 g
Protein	2.3 g
Carbohydrates	8.4 g
Cholesterol	0 mg
Fiber	0.7 g
Calories from fat	42%

1   Preheat oven to 450°F.

2   Place whole eggplants on a baking dish and roast, turning once or twice, for 45 minutes to an hour, until skin is charred and eggplant is soft. Set aside until cool enough to handle.

3   Scoop the flesh out of the eggplant and roughly mash with a fork. Stir in tahini, garlic, lemon juice, and salt. Leave it coarse or whiz it in the food processor until as smooth as you like. If necessary, thin with a little extra lemon juice or water.

4   Transfer to a bowl and drizzle with olive oil. Serve with pita chips, veggies, or grilled bread.

Makes about 3 cups.

CREAMY BABA GHANOUJ
Add a few big spoonfuls of plain (preferably Balkan-style) yogurt in the food processor.

ROASTED EGGPLANT & TOMATO DIP
Mash the roasted eggplant coarsely with a fork, drizzling with olive oil. Omit the tahini and lemon juice and stir in 1 chopped tomato, ¼ cup finely chopped purple onion, and 1 Tbsp balsamic vinegar. Top with chopped cilantro or Italian parsley.

Romesco Dip

This roasted red pepper, bread, and almond dip is similar to muhammara; all of the fat comes from healthy nuts and olive oil, and the toasted almonds and bread thicken the dip and add depth to the flavor and body to the texture. It improves after a few days in the fridge, and makes a fantastic spread for sandwiches, wraps, or pitas. It's also great thinned with a little water and served with cooked tail-on shrimp, for dipping.

¼ cup sliced or slivered almonds, or half almonds and half pine nuts

1 clove garlic, peeled

2 thick slices French bread, toasted

2 red peppers, roasted (page 78)

1 Tbsp red wine, sherry, or balsamic vinegar

½ tsp paprika

pinch dried red pepper flakes

salt to taste

4–6 Tbsp olive oil

Per ¼ cup:

Calories	151
Total fat	12.5 g
saturated fat	1.6 g
monounsaturated fat	8.7 g
polyunsaturated fat	1.6 g
Protein	2.3 g
Carbohydrates	9 g
Cholesterol	0 mg
Fiber	1.5 g
Calories from fat	71%

1 Toast almonds and garlic in a small saucepan over medium heat for about 3 minutes, until the almonds are pale golden and fragrant. Transfer to a food processor. Tear the bread into chunks into the food processor. Pulse until the bread and nuts turn to crumbs.

2 Add the red peppers, vinegar, paprika, red pepper flakes, and salt and whiz until well blended. With the motor running, slowly drizzle in the olive oil and process until the mixture has the consistency of thick mayonnaise, scraping down the sides of the bowl.

3 Serve with pitas, slices of crusty baguette, cooked tail-on shrimp, naan, or veggies.

Makes about 1½ cups.

Roasted Red Pepper & Garlic Dip

This dip is amazingly creamy considering how little fat it contains. Its flavor and texture remind me of something cheesy.

2 red bell peppers

1 head garlic

½ cup light sour cream

1–2 Tbsp olive oil

½ tsp cumin

¼ tsp salt, or to taste

pinch cayenne (optional)

Per ¼ cup:

Calories	72
Total fat	3.4 g
saturated fat	0.9 g
monounsaturated fat	1.9 g
polyunsaturated fat	0.3 g
Protein	2.2 g
Carbohydrates	9 g
Cholesterol	3.3 mg
Fiber	1 g
Calories from fat	41%

1   Preheat oven to 450°F.

2   Cut peppers in half lengthwise, clean out the ribs and seeds, and place them cut side down on a baking sheet lined with foil. Cut a thin slice off the top of the head of garlic and wrap in a piece of foil. Place on the baking sheet with the peppers and roast both until the pepper skins have blackened and blistered.

3   Remove from the oven and place the peppers in a bowl; cover with a plate, the foil from the pan, or a tea towel and set aside to cool. This will give them a chance to steam as they cool. Let the garlic cool in its foil too.

4   When they are cool enough to handle, peel the skins off the peppers and put them into the bowl of a food processor. Pour in the juices that have collected in the bottom of the bowl and squeeze the garlic cloves out of their papery skins into the bowl.

5   Add the sour cream, olive oil, cumin, salt, and cayenne (if you like) and blend until smooth. Transfer to a bowl and serve, or chill for up to 4 days; serve with veggies, pitas, or tortilla chips.

Makes about 1½ cups.

Olive Tapenade

A tapenade is a condiment from the Provence region of France typically made with olives, capers, and other seasonings. Although this version does contain less fat than traditional recipes, it's still pretty high in fat on account of the olives and olive oil—virtually all healthy monounsaturated fat, the kind we need to include more of in our diet. And because it's so intensely flavored, you need only a teeny bit. Olive tapenade makes an excellent alternative to mayo (or try mixing equal parts) on roasted chicken or veggie sandwiches, and is great tossed with hot pasta, roasted tomatoes, and crumbled feta cheese.

1 cup pitted kalamata olives or other good-quality brine-cured black olives

3 garlic cloves, peeled

2–4 anchovy fillets, or a good squeeze of anchovy paste (optional)

1–2 Tbsp capers, drained

1 tsp chopped fresh thyme (optional)

1 tsp chopped fresh rosemary

1 Tbsp lemon juice

¼ cup extra virgin olive oil

freshly ground black pepper (optional)

Per ¼ cup:

Calories	114
Total fat	12.3 g
saturated fat	1.7 g
monounsaturated fat	8.9 g
polyunsaturated fat	1.1 g
Protein	0.8 g
Carbohydrates	1.2 g
Cholesterol	1.1 mg
Fiber	1.1 g
Calories from fat	93%

1 Place olives, garlic, anchovies (if using), capers, thyme (if using), rosemary, and lemon juice in the bowl of a food processor and pulse to chop and blend. With the motor running, slowly drizzle the olive oil through the feed tube and process until puréed. Add a grinding of black pepper if you like, but because the olives, anchovies, and capers are so salty it won't need additional salt.

2 Serve with crackers or fresh breadsticks.

Makes about 1½ cups.

OLIVE & SUN-DRIED TOMATO TAPENADE
Replace ½ cup of the olives with chopped sun-dried tomatoes, and add a roasted red pepper.

MUSHROOM TAPENADE
Sauté 2–3 cups chopped mushrooms (button, cremini, shiitake, portobello, or a combination) in half the oil until golden and liquid has evaporated. Add them to the olive mixture and cut the amount of olives in half.

Fig & Olive Tapenade

Figs, olives, and walnuts go wonderfully together, so why not combine them in a tapenade? Toast walnuts in a dry frying pan, shaking them often, until fragrant.

¼ lb dried figs

½ cup pitted kalamata olives

½ cup walnuts, toasted

1 Tbsp capers, drained

1 Tbsp balsamic vinegar

1 Tbsp olive or canola oil

a few sprigs of fresh thyme or one of rosemary, leaves pulled off the stems

1 Make sure your dried figs are nice and plump; if not, pour boiling water over them and let them sit for 20 minutes or so, then drain them well. Put everything into a food processor and pulse until it is as chunky or finely blended as you like; add a little extra oil if you need some more liquid to help move it along.

Makes almost 2 cups; will keep in the fridge for a week or so.

Per tablespoon:

Calories	107
Total fat	7.4 g
saturated fat	0.7 g
monounsaturated fat	3.1 g
polyunsaturated fat	3.3 g
Protein	2.5 g
Carbohydrates	9.9 g
Cholesterol	0 mg
Fiber	2.3 g
Calories from fat	57%

Antipasto

Antipasto isn't hard, but does require a lot of chopping. Don't be tempted to shortcut with a food processor—the texture just won't be the same. This recipe will make a lot, but it freezes well, and people are always grateful to be on the receiving end of a jar. Every year we make a batch at the beginning of the holiday season to give away and serve at parties.

½–1 cup olive or canola oil, or half of each

1 small head cauliflower, separated into small florets

1 large or 2 medium purple onions, peeled and chopped

two 13 oz cans or jars pitted, sliced black olives

two 13 oz cans or jars Manzanilla olives, sliced

2 small red, yellow, or green bell peppers, seeded and chopped

three 4 oz cans small cocktail shrimp, or about ¾ lb frozen cocktail shrimp

3 cans tuna in water, drained

3½ cups ketchup

1 cup white vinegar

two 10 oz cans mushroom slices or pieces, drained

1   In a very large pot, combine the oil, cauliflower, onions, and olives and bring it all to a boil over medium-high heat. Cook, stirring often, for 5 minutes. (It's difficult to tell with all those vegetables if it's actually "boiling"; just make sure it's cooking to the point where any juices you see are bubbling.)

2   Add the remaining ingredients and heat just until it boils. If you are using jars, pour the hot antipasto into hot, sterilized jars; seal and cool. Otherwise, remove the pot from the heat and let the antipasto cool, then transfer to containers to store in the fridge or freezer.

Makes about 7 quarts (28 cups).

Per ¼ cup:

Calories	43
Total fat	2.8 g
saturated fat	0.4 g
monounsaturated fat	1.9 g
polyunsaturated fat	0.3 g
Protein	2 g
Carbohydrates	3.4 g
Cholesterol	5.6 mg
Fiber	1 g
Calories from fat	54%

Green Goddess Dip

This classic dip is made green by puréed parsley, green onions, and chives—add more or less to suit your taste. The anchovies are optional, but add a flavor reminiscent of Caesar dressing.

¼ cup white wine or white balsamic vinegar

½–1 cup chopped fresh parsley (stems removed)

3 green onions, chopped

small bunch fresh chives, chopped

1 tsp–1 Tbsp anchovy paste (optional)

1–2 garlic cloves, crushed

1 Tbsp lemon juice (or to taste)

¼ tsp salt

¼ tsp freshly ground black pepper

1 cup low-fat mayonnaise

1 Purée the vinegar, parsley, green onions, chives, anchovy paste (if you like), garlic, lemon juice, and salt and pepper in the bowl of a food processor until smooth; blend in the mayonnaise. Refrigerate until ready to serve.

Makes about 2 cups.

GREEN GODDESS GUACAMOLE

Add a mashed ripe avocado to the mixture before adding the mayonnaise.

Per tablespoon:

Calories	23
Total fat	1.9 g
saturated fat	0.1 g
monounsaturated fat	1.1 g
polyunsaturated fat	0.5 g
Protein	0.1 g
Carbohydrates	1.7 g
Cholesterol	0 mg
Fiber	0.1 g
Calories from fat	70%

Spicy Tuna Schmear

This is made with those little cans of flavored tuna, which are packed in water but have tons of flavor. I usually spread this on bagels, but I've recently discovered it's great to spread on a flour tortilla (page 41) with fresh veggies on top and rolled up into a portable wrap.

half an 8 oz tub light cream cheese

2 Tbsp light mayonnaise

one 3 oz can flavored tuna, such as spicy Thai

¼ cup finely chopped celery

¼ cup finely chopped red bell pepper

salt and pepper to taste

Per tablespoon:

Calories	19
Total fat	1.3 g
saturated fat	0.6 g
monounsaturated fat	0.5 g
polyunsaturated fat	0.1 g
Protein	1.5 g
Carbohydrates	0.5 g
Cholesterol	3.6 mg
Fiber	0 g
Calories from fat	59%

1 In a medium bowl, beat the cream cheese and mayonnaise until well blended and smooth. Stir in the tuna, celery, red pepper, and salt and pepper.

2 Spread on mini bagels or serve in a bowl alongside bagel chips or crostini.

Makes about 1½ cups.

CURRIED CRAB SCHMEAR
Replace the tuna with a can of drained crabmeat, and add ½ tsp curry powder or paste and a drop or two of Tabasco sauce.

Goat Cheese Gratin with Roasted Peppers, Tomatoes & Chilies

This wonderful, warm gratin is best served with fresh olive bread or baguette. It's a bit higher in fat on account of the goat cheese; cut the amount of cheese in half if you want to cut back on fat and calories.

1 red bell pepper

1 orange or yellow bell pepper

olive or canola oil

1 pint cherry or grape tomatoes or 4 Roma tomatoes, halved

2–4 red chili peppers, seeded and chopped

3–4 garlic cloves, peeled

½ cup black olives, pitted

basil or rosemary (optional)

2 Tbsp red wine vinegar

salt, to taste (optional)

10 oz soft goat cheese

Per serving:

Calories	199
Total fat	14 g
saturated fat	8.9 g
monounsaturated fat	3.8 g
polyunsaturated fat	0.5 g
Protein	12 g
Carbohydrates	7.4 g
Cholesterol	37.2 mg
Fiber	1.8 g
Calories from fat	62%

1 Preheat oven to 450°F.

2 Seed the peppers and cut them in half. Set them cut side down on a rimmed baking sheet that has been drizzled with olive or canola oil. In a medium bowl, toss the tomatoes, chili peppers, and garlic with another drizzle of oil, toss to coat and spread them out on the pan among the peppers. Roast for 30–45 minutes, until the skin on the peppers blisters and blackens.

3 Remove the vegetables from the oven and transfer the roasted bell peppers to a bowl; cover and let stand until cool enough to handle. Scrape the roasted tomatoes, chilies, and garlic into the bowl of a food processor, along with any juices and the blacked bits on the pan. When the peppers are cool, peel off their skins and add the flesh to the food processor, along with any juices that have accumulated at the bottom of the bowl. Add the olives, some basil or rosemary if you like, and the vinegar and pulse until the mixture is well blended but still chunky. Taste and add salt, if it needs it—the olives are often salty enough.

4 Crumble the goat cheese into a shallow baking dish and spread the pepper mixture overtop. Broil for 10 minutes or until heated through and bubbly around the edges. Serve with fresh bread, pitas, or crackers.

Serves 8 (depending on appetites).

Fruit Dips

Fruit can always use a dip too; for a great summertime snack or dessert, thread chunks of fresh pineapple, apple, banana, peaches, strawberries, and mango on bamboo skewers to make fruit kebabs and serve alongside any of these dips. If you like, quickly grill them on a well-oiled barbecue first. Cubes of pound cake go really well between the fruit too.

STRAWBERRY FRUIT DIP

Blend 1 package frozen, thawed strawberries in a food processor or blender until smooth. Blend in a cup of vanilla yogurt.

SOUR CREAM WITH BROWN SUGAR

Stir about 2 Tbsp of brown sugar into 1–2 cups low-fat sour cream. Let sit until it melts, then stir again. For a creamy espresso dip, stir in 1 tsp instant espresso powder as well.

CREAMY PUMPKIN DIP

Beat half a package of low-fat cream cheese until smooth; beat in ¼ cup packed brown sugar, 2 Tbsp maple syrup, ½ cup pumpkin purée, and a pinch of cinnamon. Serve with sliced apples.

MARSHMALLOW-PEACH DIP

Stir together ¼ cup peach jam, half an 8 oz tub spreadable light cream cheese, and a jar of marshmallow crème.

DULCE DE LECHE

Pour 2 cans of low-fat sweetened condensed milk into a pie plate and cover with foil. Bake at 425°F for an hour and a half, until it's thick and golden. Stir in ½ tsp vanilla and a pinch of salt. For Rum Dulce de Leche, stir in ¼ cup dark rum, too.

CREAMY KEY LIME DIP

Stir together a can of low-fat sweetened condensed milk and ½ cup lime juice (Key lime juice if you can get it). This goes well with graham crackers for dipping.

CHOCOLATE FONDUE

Warm a can of Hershey's chocolate syrup on the stovetop, and stir in ½ lb chopped semi-sweet chocolate until it melts.

Finger-Lickin' Food

The best foods, I think, are the kinds that require a lot of napkins and finger licking.

They aren't the best choice for parties that call for fancy clothes, but they are perfect for any occasion at which you won't be embarrassed if you have to lick off your hands, and maybe even your arm. Kids are fans of finger foods too—crunchy chicken fingers, pizza, cheese sticks, and buffalo chicken drumsticks are always well received, especially when served restaurant-style on a big platter with some fresh veggies and dip to round out the meal. No one will realize they're eating healthier, so don't bother telling them.

Chicken Strips with Honey Mustard

This is a fantastically versatile recipe; no matter what you have in your cupboard, as long as you have chicken you will likely be able to come up with some form of crumbs to make these. Panko—extra crunchy Japanese crumbs that create a wonderful crust—is available at Asian markets and gourmet stores. If you're not a fan of honey mustard, try bottled plum sauce for dipping.

3 skinless, boneless chicken breasts or
1 turkey breast (about 1 lb)

1 large egg or ½ cup buttermilk

1 cup(ish) panko (Japanese breadcrumbs),
corn flake crumbs, dry breadcrumbs, or finely
crushed crackers

¼ cup grated Parmesan cheese or ground
pecans (optional)

salt and pepper to taste

honey and mustard, for dipping

Per serving:

Calories	264
Total fat	4.6 g
saturated fat	2 g
monounsaturated fat	1.4 g
polyunsaturated fat	0.5 g
Protein	32 g
Carbohydrates	20.9 g
Cholesterol	124.6 mg
Fiber	0.6 g
Calories from fat	16%

1 Cut your chicken or turkey into strips any size you like (keep them fairly uniform if you want them to cook evenly). If you're using buttermilk, put the chicken into a bowl or Ziploc bag and pour the buttermilk overtop; refrigerate for an hour or up to 24 hours (or freeze for up to 4 months). Otherwise, stir the egg with a fork in a shallow dish, just to break it up. Combine the crumbs, Parmesan cheese (or any other additions), and salt and pepper in another shallow dish.

2 Preheat the oven to 375°F.

3 Dip the chicken strips into the egg (or remove from the buttermilk) and dredge in the crumbs to coat well. Place about an inch apart on a baking sheet that has been sprayed with nonstick spray. (If you want, lightly spray the strips with cooking spray as well—this will help them brown a little better). Bake for 15–20 minutes, until golden and cooked through.

4 Alternatively, cook the coated chicken strips in a little canola or olive oil in a frying pan set over medium-high heat, flipping as necessary until golden and cooked through. Mix equal amounts of honey and mustard for dipping.

Serves 4.

CURRIED ALMOND CHICKEN FINGERS

Coat chicken strips in a mixture of 1½ cups crumbs, ½ cup finely chopped or ground almonds, and 1 tsp curry powder.

PECAN-CRUSTED CHICKEN FINGERS

Coat chicken strips in a mixture of ¾ cup finely chopped pecans, ½ cup corn flakes or panko crumbs, 2 Tbsp flour, and a bit of salt and pepper.

SPICY CHICKEN FINGERS

Add 1 Tbsp chili powder to the crumb mixture, and a few drops of Tabasco sauce to the buttermilk or egg.

FALAFEL CHICKEN FINGERS

Dredge the chicken in egg or buttermilk, then in a dry falafel mix before cooking.

Barbecue Buffalo Chicken Strips with Blue Cheese Dip

The classic formula for restaurant-style buffalo wings sauce is half butter, half hot sauce; using barbecue sauce cuts back dramatically on the fat and calories! If you want to make them in advance, you can freeze the dipped chicken strips on a baking sheet, then transfer to a plastic bag. When you're ready to bake them, place the frozen strips on a baking sheet and bake as directed—there's no need to thaw them first. If you want to skip the blue cheese dip, bottled low-fat ranch or creamy cucumber dressing makes great dips too.

1 lb skinless, boneless chicken or turkey breasts, cut into strips

¼ cup flour

salt and pepper to taste

½ cup barbecue sauce

¼ cup hot sauce (such as Frank's RedHot Sauce)

Blue Cheese Dip

½ cup low-fat sour cream or plain yogurt

2 Tbsp light mayonnaise

2 oz blue cheese, crumbled

1 green onion, finely chopped

1   Preheat oven to 400°F.

2   Season flour with salt and pepper in a shallow dish. Stir together the barbecue sauce and hot sauce in another dish.

3   Dredge chicken strips in the flour to coat, then dip into the barbecue sauce mixture and turn to coat all over. Place on a baking sheet that has been sprayed with nonstick spray. Bake for 20 minutes, or until cooked through.

4   To make the blue cheese dip, stir together all the dip ingredients. Serve the chicken strips warm, with blue cheese dip.

Makes about 1 dozen strips and ¾ cup dip.

Per strip + tablespoon of dip:

Calories	60	+ 3.6
Total fat	0.9 g	+ 2.5 g
saturated fat	0.2 g	+ 1.2 g
monounsaturated fat	0.2 g	+ 0.9 g
polyunsaturated fat	0.2 g	+ 0.3 g
Protein	8.9 g	+ 1.6 g
Carbohydrates	3.4 g	+ 1.7 g
Cholesterol	21.9 mg	+ 5.2 mg
Fiber	0.7 g	+ 0 g
Calories from fat	14%	+ 63%

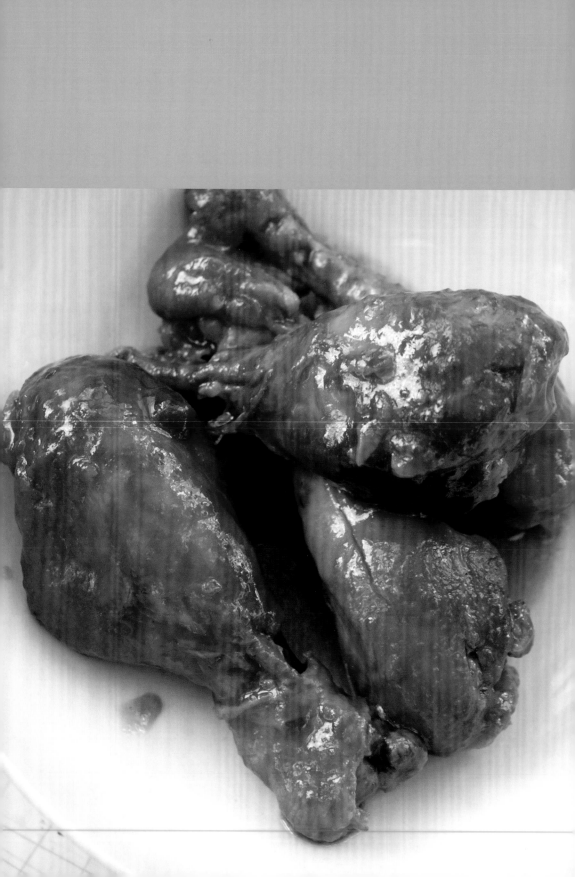

Sticky, Spicy Drumsticks

The ultimate finger foods, I think, are those that require a lot of finger licking. Chicken wings are the best for this, but they are all skin, which is where virtually all the fat is. Skinned drumsticks are far better than wings—much more meat, no skin, and you can still eat it off the bone with your fingers. These are reminiscent of sweet-and-sour chicken, but with a spicy kick. Use less hot sauce if you're feeding kids; more if you like the heat. Cook them under the broiler or throw them on the grill for a smokier flavor.

8 chicken drumsticks, skinned and trimmed of any fat

½ cup ketchup

¼ cup honey

¼ cup rice vinegar

2 Tbsp brown sugar

1 Tbsp soy sauce

1 Tbsp Worcestershire sauce

1 Tbsp Tabasco or other hot sauce

2–3 garlic cloves, crushed

1   Combine everything but the drumsticks in a medium bowl. Add the drumsticks and stir to coat.

2   Grill or broil the drumsticks, brushing with marinade, for about 20 minutes or until cooked through. If there is extra marinade, bring it to a boil in a small pot and simmer for a minute, until thoroughly cooked. Serve with the drumsticks for dipping.

Makes 8 drumsticks.

BUFFALO DRUMSTICKS
Combine ¼ cup Tabasco or other hot sauce, 2 Tbsp melted butter, 1 Tbsp red wine vinegar, ½ tsp paprika, and ½ tsp salt for the marinade. Serve with Blue Cheese Dip (page 94).

Per drumstick:

Calories	144
Total fat	2.2 g
saturated fat	0.6 g
monounsaturated fat	0.7 g
polyunsaturated fat	0.6 g
Protein	13.3 g
Carbohydrates	18.6 g
Cholesterol	47.7 mg
Fiber	0.3 g
Calories from fat	13%

Cheese Sticks

Who isn't a fan of gooey, crispy cheese? Although these are baked rather than deep-fried, they are every bit as good as the ones you order in a restaurant. If you have kids around, they will love them.

8 part-skim mozzarella cheese strings

2 Tbsp flour

1 large egg, lightly beaten with a fork

1 cup panko (Japanese breadcrumbs), dry breadcrumbs, or cracker crumbs

salt and pepper to taste

spaghetti or pizza sauce or salsa, for dipping (about ½ cup)

Per stick:

Calories	64
Total fat	2.6 g
saturated fat	0.2 g
monounsaturated fat	0.3 g
polyunsaturated fat	0.2 g
Protein	4.4 g
Carbohydrates	5.6 g
Cholesterol	13.5 mg
Fiber	0.4 g
Calories from fat	37%

1 Place the cheese strings in the freezer at least an hour before you plan to make these if you can—they tend to ooze less when they're nice and cold to begin with. Preheat the oven to 400°F.

2 Place the flour, egg, and crumbs in 3 separate bowls. Season the flour with salt and pepper. Cut the cheese strings in half widthwise. Dip 1 cheese stick at a time into the flour to coat, then into the egg, and then the crumbs. Dip it into the egg again, and again into the crumbs, squeezing to help them adhere. It'll be messy, but try to cover the cheese completely. Place on a baking sheet that has been sprayed with nonstick spray. Repeat with the remaining cheese sticks.

3 Bake for 10–15 minutes, until golden. Serve immediately. Warm up the spaghetti sauce and serve alongside for dipping.

Makes 16 sticks.

Mini "Toad-in-the-Hole"

Toad-in-the-hole is a traditional British dish made by pouring Yorkshire pudding batter over pork sausages and baking it until the batter rises up crisp and crunchy around the sausage. These are bite sized, so you're guaranteed some sausage and some pud in each bite. Unlike traditional toad-in-the-hole, these are remarkably low in fat. Like the traditional version, they are just as good at midnight as they are at breakfast or brunch.

6 small or 3 large lean chicken sausages (about ⅓ lb)

½ cup flour

½ cup milk

1 large egg

salt and pepper to taste

grainy mustard, for serving

Per piece:

Calories	32
Total fat	0.8 g
saturated fat	0.3 g
monounsaturated fat	0.4 g
polyunsaturated fat	0.1 g
Protein	2.6 g
Carbohydrates	3.5 g
Cholesterol	20 mg
Fiber	0.1 g
Calories from fat	23%

1 Preheat oven to 350°F.

2 Cut the sausages into 1-inch pieces. Spray a mini muffin pan with nonstick spray (use 2 pans if you have them) and put a piece of sausage into each cup, standing it upright if you can. Bake for about 10 minutes, until they're beginning to brown. Turn the oven up to 450°F, leaving the sausages inside.

3 In a medium bowl, whisk together the flour, milk, egg, and salt and pepper until relatively smooth.

4 Remove the sausages from the oven and quickly pour a scant tablespoon of batter around each sausage. Return the pan to the oven for 15–20 minutes, until puffed and golden. Serve them warm, a dab of grainy mustard dabbed on top or a dish served alongside.

Makes about 16 mini toad-in-the-holes.

MINI YORKSHIRE PUDDINGS WITH ROAST BEEF & HORSERADISH CREAM
Bake the batter in the muffin cups without the sausage. Top each mini Yorkshire pudding with a little pile of thinly sliced deli roast beef. Stir 1–2 Tbsp prepared horseradish or grainy mustard into a cup of low-fat sour cream and top each piece with a small dollop of it.

Goong Waan (Sweet & Spicy Shrimp)

This is a variation of a recipe from Sheila Lukins's wonderful *All Around the World Cookbook*. She credits it to a cooking class in Bangkok. Make sure you use peeled shrimp with the tails left on to use as a handle—if you use shrimp in their shells, the shells fuse to the meat!

1 lb large tail-on shrimp

¼ cup water

½ cup packed brown sugar

3 Tbsp fish sauce

2 garlic cloves, crushed

¼ tsp ground white pepper

chopped fresh cilantro, for sprinkling

Per serving:

Calories	226
Total fat	2 g
saturated fat	0.4 g
monounsaturated fat	0.3 g
polyunsaturated fat	0.8 g
Protein	23.1 g
Carbohydrates	28.3 g
Cholesterol	172.4 mg
Fiber	0 g
Calories from fat	8%

1. In a medium saucepan, combine the water, brown sugar, and fish sauce. Cook over medium heat for a few minutes until the sugar dissolves.

2. Add the garlic and pepper and bring to a boil. Reduce heat and simmer until the sauce reduces and thickens, about 8–10 minutes.

3. Add the shrimp and cook, stirring and flipping them constantly, just until they turn pink. This should take only a minute or two. Transfer to a bowl, sprinkle with cilantro, and set aside to cool.

4. Refrigerate shrimp until chilled, and transfer to a serving bowl with a slotted spoon. Serve with lots of napkins and an extra bowl for the tails.

Serves 4.

Curried Orange-Peanut Shrimp

Throw the shrimp and marinade into a baggie in the morning and you'll have dinner almost ready when you come home from work. Sometimes I simmer the whole lot, sauce and all, in a large frying pan and serve it over rice. (If you do this, try doubling the sauce and adding a handful of torn fresh spinach at the end, just until it wilts.)

¼ cup orange marmalade

¼ cup orange juice

2–4 Tbsp peanut butter (preferably all-natural)

1 tsp curry paste

1 tsp sesame or canola oil

1 garlic clove, crushed

½ tsp chili sauce or sambal oelek

¼ tsp salt

pinch red pepper flakes

½ lb large shrimp, peeled and deveined, with the tails left on

Per serving:

Calories	177
Total fat	6.2 g
saturated fat	1.1 g
monounsaturated fat	2.5 g
polyunsaturated fat	2 g
Protein	13.2 g
Carbohydrates	17.8 g
Cholesterol	86.2 mg
Fiber	0.7 g
Calories from fat	31%

1 Combine everything but the shrimp in a bowl or jar and whisk or shake until smooth. Pour over the shrimp in a container or Ziploc bag and marinate in the fridge for an hour or overnight.

2 When ready to cook, spray a large non-stick sauté pan with nonstick spray and set over medium heat. Add the shrimp and cook for a few minutes on each side, just until they turn pink. (If you want, you could thread the shrimp onto bamboo skewers that have been soaked in water; place on a grill rack or broiler pan that has been sprayed with non-stick spray and cook for about 2 minutes on each side.) Simmer the reserved marinade in a small saucepan for a few minutes and serve alongside the shrimp for dipping.

Serves 4.

Potato Skins

This may seem like an obvious recipe, but cheesy potato skins are a quintessential finger food and people don't often make them at home. The spice mixture adds a lot of flavor, and Canadian bacon is much leaner than the breakfast variety. I always use intensely flavored cheeses, like old cheddar, instead of the low-fat kind, which tends to be rubbery with very little flavor.

4 medium baking potatoes (russets work well and have sturdy skins)

1–2 Tbsp olive or canola oil

¼ tsp each salt and pepper

½ tsp each chili powder and curry powder (optional)

¼ cup chopped Canadian bacon or turkey pepperoni

2 green onions, chopped

¾ cup grated old cheddar cheese

salsa and low-fat sour cream

Per serving:

Calories	170
Total fat	7.2 g
saturated fat	2.8 g
monounsaturated fat	3.6 g
polyunsaturated fat	0.4 g
Protein	6.8 g
Carbohydrates	20.4 g
Cholesterol	16 mg
Fiber	2.3 g
Calories from fat	38%

1 Preheat oven to 400°F.

2 Bake the potatoes whole for about an hour, until tender. Set aside until cool enough to handle.

3 Cut each potato in quarters lengthwise and scoop out the pulp, leaving a ¼-inch-thick shell. (Keep the pulp for something else—I always fry it up in a little oil the next morning with whatever's left of the spice mixture for amazing home fries!) Place potato skins on a baking sheet and brush with oil. Combine the salt and pepper, and the chili and curry powders (if you like) and sprinkle overtop. Bake for another 10 minutes, until crispy.

4 Sprinkle with bacon, green onions, and cheese, and bake for another 5 minutes, until the cheese melts. Serve with salsa and low-fat sour cream.

Serves 4.

Green Eggs with Ham

Okay, so I came up with this recipe just so I could use the name. But it turned out to be one of my favorites! Spinach, eggs, ham, and cheese are a great combo. These are really intensely flavored little bites.

6 large eggs

1 tsp canola oil

2 slices deli ham, chopped

a handful of fresh spinach or chard, chopped

1 Tbsp light mayonnaise

2 Tbsp grated Parmesan cheese

salt and pepper to taste

Per egg half:

Calories	55
Total fat	3.7 g
saturated fat	1.1 g
monounsaturated fat	1.5 g
polyunsaturated fat	0.6 g
Protein	4.5 g
Carbohydrates	0.8 g
Cholesterol	111 mg
Fiber	0.1 g
Calories from fat	61%

1 Place the eggs in a medium saucepan. Cover with water and bring to a boil. Cover, remove from heat, and let stand 15 minutes. Drain and rinse with cold water until cool. Peel and slice in half lengthwise. Remove yolks and set 3 aside for another use, or feed them to your dog.

2 Meanwhile, heat the oil in a saucepan set over medium heat and sauté the ham for a minute. Add the spinach and cook for another minute, until wilted.

3 In a medium bowl mash the 3 yolks with the mayonnaise, Parmesan cheese, and salt and pepper until smooth. Add the spinach mixture and stir until well blended.

4 Stuff egg white halves with filling and serve immediately.

Makes 12.

Smoked Salmon Deviled Eggs

It seems everyone gets excited over deviled eggs—at a party they're always the first to go.

Eggs aren't as bad for you as you might think—they are lower in cholesterol than was once thought, and of the 5 grams of fat a large yolk contains, only 1 is saturated. These recipes eliminate half the yolks and replace them with more flavorful ingredients.

1 small Yukon gold potato, peeled and diced

6 large eggs

½ cup crumbled smoked or barbecue salmon tip

1 Tbsp light mayonnaise

1 tsp fresh lemon juice

1 tsp grainy mustard

1 green onion or a small bunch of chives, finely chopped

salt and pepper to taste

Per egg:

Calories	65
Total fat	3.4 g
saturated fat	0.9 g
monounsaturated fat	1.3 g
polyunsaturated fat	0.6 g
Protein	5.8 g
Carbohydrates	2.9 g
Cholesterol	114 mg
Fiber	0.3 g
Calories from fat	47%

1   Cook the potato in a pot of boiling salted water until very tender. Drain and cool.

2   Meanwhile, place the eggs in a medium saucepan. Cover with water and bring to a boil. Cover, remove from heat, and let stand 15 minutes. Drain and rinse with cold water until cool. Peel and slice in half lengthwise. Remove yolks and set 3 aside for another use, or feed them to your dog.

3   In a medium bowl combine the remaining yolks, potato, salmon, mayonnaise, lemon juice, and mustard; mash with a fork until well blended. Stir in the green onion and salt and pepper.

4   Stuff egg white halves with filling and chill until ready to serve.

Makes 12.

California Rolls (Sushi with Avocado & Crab)

I'm not very daring when it comes to sushi—I usually stick to California rolls while my friends tuck in to sashimi and barbecued eel. I discovered after a friend took a sushi-making class that California rolls aren't very difficult to make. They are also very delicious and very low in calories. You'll need a bamboo sushi mat, which is available at most kitchen stores for a few dollars.

1 cup long-grain rice or sushi rice

¼ cup rice vinegar

1 Tbsp sugar

1 tsp salt

1 avocado, peeled, pitted, and cut into long, thin slices, or 1 small English cucumber, peeled, seeded, and cut into long, thin slices

2 Tbsp lemon juice

½ lb crab meat or imitation crab (pollock)

¼ cup light mayonnaise (optional)

6 sheets nori (seaweed)

soy sauce, wasabi, and pickled ginger, for serving

Per piece:

Calories	37
Total fat	1 g
saturated fat	0.2 g
monounsaturated fat	0.6 g
polyunsaturated fat	0.2 g
Protein	1.8 g
Carbohydrates	5.2 g
Cholesterol	3.3 mg
Fiber	0.2 g
Calories from fat	24%

1   Rinse the rice in cold water until the water runs clear. Drain well and combine with 1½ cups water in a heavy saucepan. Let stand for 30 minutes, then bring to a boil, cover, and simmer over low heat for 10 minutes. Turn the heat up to high for another minute and then remove from heat. Let stand, covered, for 15 more minutes and then transfer the rice to a bowl.

2   Combine the vinegar, sugar, and salt in a small saucepan and cook until the sugar is dissolved. Cool and add to the warm rice, stirring gently. Cool completely.

3   Toss the avocado with lemon juice to prevent discoloring, and toss the crabmeat with mayonnaise (if using). Lay a bamboo sushi mat on the counter and put a piece of the nori on it with a long side facing you. With dampened hands, spread about ½ cup of the rice over it, leaving a 1-inch border across the top edge.

4   Arrange 3 avocado slices across the middle of the rice along with one-sixth of the crab. Grab the edge of the nori and mat and roll the nori away from you as tightly as you can, pressing the roll as you go to keep its shape. Moisten the edge of the nori and press to seal. Transfer to a cutting board and cut rolls to 1-inch pieces. Make 5 more rolls. Serve with soy sauce, wasabi, and pickled ginger.

Makes 36 pieces.

Balsamic Mushroom Crostini

If you can sauté a pan of mushrooms and toast bread, you can make these crostini. The mushrooms are accessorized with rosemary, cranberries, and a splash of balsamic vinegar, then topped with flavorful cheese and popped back into the oven until the cheese melts.

1 thin baguette, sliced diagonally about ¼ inch thick (you'll need only 20 or so slices)

1 large garlic clove, cut in half lengthwise

1 Tbsp olive or canola oil (for sautéing mushrooms)

1 Tbsp butter

6 cups sliced fresh mushrooms—button, portobello, shiitake, or a combination

⅓ cup dried cranberries or chopped dried cherries

2 Tbsp balsamic vinegar or red wine

1 Tbsp chopped fresh rosemary or thyme

salt and pepper to taste

½–1 cup grated aged Gouda, Asiago, fontina, or old white cheddar cheese

Per crostini:

Calories	76
Total fat	3.4 g
saturated fat	1.6 g
monounsaturated fat	1.3 g
polyunsaturated fat	0.2 g
Protein	3 g
Carbohydrates	8.7 g
Cholesterol	8.7 mg
Fiber	0.7 g
Calories from fat	39%

1 Preheat oven to 400°F.

2 Place baguette slices on a baking sheet (if you like, brush them lightly with olive oil before baking) and toast in the oven for about 10 minutes, until barely golden. Remove from the oven and rub each with a cut clove of garlic.

3 Heat the oil and butter in a large frying pan set over medium-high heat. When the foam subsides, cook the mushrooms, stirring occasionally, until the moisture has evaporated. Continue to cook until the mushrooms are golden. Add the cranberries, balsamic vinegar, and rosemary and cook for another minute, until the liquid has evaporated. Season with salt and pepper.

4 Spoon the hot mixture onto toasts and sprinkle with cheese. Return to the oven for 5 minutes, until the cheese melts.

Makes about 20 crostini.

BALSAMIC MUSHROOM DIP
Finely chop the mushrooms before you cook them. Omit the grated cheese and stir 4 oz light cream cheese or soft goat cheese and ½ cup light sour cream into the finished mixture on the stovetop; turn the heat to low and stir until the cheese melts. Serve warm with crackers or crostini for dipping.

Bruschetta

The term bruschetta (pronounced either *brusketta* or *brushetta*) traditionally refers to toasted bread rubbed with garlic and drizzled with olive oil. But in Canada when someone says "bruschetta," they are more often referring to a salsa-like mixture of tomatoes, garlic, and oil served on a slice of toasted baguette (or bruschetta!). Use as much or as little oil as suits your taste.

4 ripe tomatoes, diced

1–2 garlic cloves, finely crushed

1–4 Tbsp extra virgin olive oil

1 Tbsp balsamic vinegar

¼ cup finely chopped fresh basil (optional)

salt and freshly ground pepper to taste

18 crostini (page 40) or toasted baguette slices

Per piece:

Calories	40
Total fat	1.1 g
saturated fat	0.2 g
monounsaturated fat	0.7 g
polyunsaturated fat	0.2 g
Protein	1.1 g
Carbohydrates	6.6 g
Cholesterol	0 mg
Fiber	0.6 g
Calories from fat	24%

1   Mix everything but the crostini together in a large bowl. Spoon onto crostini or serve it in a bowl alongside the crostini so people can serve themselves.

Makes about 18 pieces.

SMASHED CHERRY TOMATO & OLIVE BRUSCHETTA
Use a pint of cherry tomatoes and ¼ cup of pitted kalamata olives, and smash them with a potato masher until roughly mashed. Add the garlic, oil, vinegar, basil, salt, and pepper.

White Bean, Tomato & Olive Bruschetta with Goat Cheese

Bring a container of this bruschetta and a chunk of baguette to work for lunch, or to the park or beach for a picnic. To get the pits out of olives, smash them on a board with the flat side of your knife; they will split open, allowing easy access to the pits.

one 19 oz can white kidney beans, rinsed and drained

3 ripe plum tomatoes, seeded and chopped

¼–½ cup kalamata olives, pitted and chopped

¼ cup chopped fresh basil

2 Tbsp olive oil

1 Tbsp balsamic vinegar

2 garlic cloves, crushed

salt and pepper to taste

24 crostini (page 40) or toasted baguette slices

4 oz soft fresh goat cheese, crumbled feta, or grated Parmesan

1 In a medium bowl, lightly mash the beans with a fork, keeping them chunky. Stir in the tomatoes, olives, basil, olive oil, vinegar, garlic, and salt and pepper. Stir until well blended.

2 If you are using goat cheese, spread it on the toasts and spoon the bean mixture on top. If you are using feta or Parmesan cheese, spoon the bean mixture onto the toasts and sprinkle the grated cheese on top. Pop them into the oven until the cheese melts if you like.

Makes about 2 dozen pieces.

Per piece:

Calories	92
Total fat	3.4 g
saturated fat	1.4 g
monounsaturated fat	1.5 g
polyunsaturated fat	0.3 g
Protein	4.4 g
Carbohydrates	11 g
Cholesterol	5 mg
Fiber	2 g
Calories from fat	33%

Chicken, Black Bean & Mushroom Quesadillas

If you can make a grilled cheese sandwich, you can make a quesadilla! They are a little trickier to flip—if you have trouble, slide the quesadilla onto a plate, and then invert it back into the pan, or make folded quesadillas by using one tortilla at a time and flipping half of it over the filling like an omelet.

People tend to get more creative with their fillings when making quesadillas than with grilled cheese. Basically, you can put anything inside—just make sure there is enough cheese to keep it together.

1 tsp canola oil or butter

1 small onion, finely chopped

2 cups sliced mushrooms

2 garlic cloves, crushed (optional)

½ cup chopped cooked chicken

half a 19 oz can black beans, rinsed and drained

½ tsp ground cumin

salt to taste

six 10-inch flour tortillas (page 41)

1–1½ cups grated old cheddar cheese

Per serving:

Calories	284
Total fat	8.7 g
saturated fat	3.6 g
monounsaturated fat	2.9 g
polyunsaturated fat	1.6 g
Protein	17.4 g
Carbohydrates	34.2 g
Cholesterol	30.6 mg
Fiber	5 g
Calories from fat	27%

1. Heat the oil in a large frying pan set over medium heat and sauté the onions for a few minutes, until soft. Add the mushrooms and garlic (if using) and cook until the mushrooms are golden and the moisture has evaporated. Add the chicken, beans, cumin, and salt and stir until well blended. Remove from heat.

2. Place a flour tortilla in a large dry frying pan set over medium heat and spread with a quarter of the cheese, half the chicken mixture, and another quarter of the cheese. Top with a second tortilla. Cook, shaking the pan gently and pressing the top to help it seal, until the bottom is golden and the cheese is melting. If you don't feel confident flipping the quesadilla, slide it onto a plate and invert it back into the pan. Cook for another few minutes, until golden on the other side and the cheese is melted. Slide onto a plate and repeat with the remaining tortillas, chicken, and cheese.

3. Cut into wedges and serve with salsa and light sour cream.

   Serves 6.

Pizza Dough

Everyone should be able to make a good pizza crust. This is as easy as it gets. If you're in a hurry, use instant yeast to speed up rising time; if you're not, let the dough rise in the fridge overnight (the cold will slow the rising dough) or freeze for up to 4 months. Once you get the hang of pizza dough, it will take under 10 minutes to stir up a batch. If there are kids around, ask them to help knead.

Add about a teaspoon of dried Italian seasoning, oregano, basil, or chopped rosemary; a crushed clove of garlic; and a few finely chopped olives or sun-dried tomatoes as you stir together the wet and dry ingredients. If you use sun-dried tomatoes packed in oil, use that oil in place of the olive oil.

1 cup lukewarm water

1 pkg (or 2¼ tsp) active dry yeast

1 tsp sugar or honey

2½–3 cups flour; all-purpose, whole wheat, or a combination (I usually use about 2¾ cups in total)

1 tsp salt

1 Tbsp olive or canola oil

Per slice (6 slices per pizza), made with half whole wheat and half all-purpose flour:

Calories	112
Total fat	1.6 g
saturated fat	0.2 g
monounsaturated fat	0.7 g
polyunsaturated fat	0.5 g
Protein	3.7 g
Carbohydrates	21.4 g
Cholesterol	0 mg
Fiber	2.5 g
Calories from fat	12%

1   In a large bowl, stir together the water, yeast, and sugar; set aside for 5 minutes, until it's foamy. Add 2½ cups of the flour, salt, and oil and stir until the dough comes together. On a lightly floured surface, knead the dough for about 8 minutes, until it's smooth and elastic, adding a little more flour if the dough is too sticky.

2   Place the dough in an oiled bowl and turn to coat all over. Cover with a tea towel or plastic wrap and set aside in a warm place for about an hour, until doubled in bulk. If you want you can let it rise more slowly in the refrigerator for up to 8 hours.

3   Punch the dough down, cover again, and let it rest for 5 minutes. Divide it in half and shape each into a circle (or make individual mini pizzas) and place on a baking sheet that has been sprinkled with cornmeal.

4   Let the crust rise another half hour while you prepare the toppings. Spread the pizza dough with tomato sauce, sprinkle with desired toppings, and bake at 450°F for 15–20 minutes, until bubbly and golden.

Makes enough dough for two 9-inch pizzas.

Caramelized Onion, Olive & Feta Pizza

Pizza dough doubles easily and freezes well, so if you want only one pizza, freeze half the dough for later. If you need to feed a crowd, double the recipe.

1 batch pizza dough (page 115)

1 Tbsp olive or canola oil

2–3 large onions, halved and thinly sliced

1 clove garlic, crushed

1 Tbsp balsamic vinegar

freshly ground black pepper

1 cup (about 4 oz) crumbled feta or goat cheese

¼ cup coarsely chopped pitted kalamata olives

Per piece (based on 12 slices):

Calories	176
Total fat	4.4 g
saturated fat	1.8 g
monounsaturated fat	1.8 g
polyunsaturated fat	0.5 g
Protein	5.4 g
Carbohydrates	28.8 g
Cholesterol	8.7 mg
Fiber	2.3 g
Calories from fat	22%

1. Preheat oven to 350°F.

2. In a large frying pan, sauté the onions in the oil over medium heat for about 10 minutes, until golden. Stir in the garlic and cook for another minute; add the balsamic vinegar and pepper and cook until the liquid has evaporated.

3. Spread the caramelized onions on the unbaked pizza crusts and sprinkle with feta and olives. Bake for 15–20 minutes, until golden and the cheese melts.

Makes 2 pizzas.

SAUSAGE, CARAMELIZED ONION, OLIVE & FETA PIZZA

Crumble a hot or mild Italian sausage into the frying pan and cook, breaking up with a spoon, until cooked through. Remove the sausage from the frying pan and sauté the onions in the drippings in the pan. Sprinkle the crumbled sausage over the crust along with the caramelized onions.

Barbecue Chicken Pizza

Pizza doesn't have to be made with tomato sauce—try bottled barbecue sauce or pesto for something new. If you don't have mozzarella, use up any bits of cheese you have lurking in the fridge.

1 batch pizza dough (page 115)

1 cup chopped roasted chicken

½ cup barbecue sauce (or to taste)

2 cups grated part-skim mozzarella cheese, cheddar, Gouda, or a combination

1 green onion, chopped

2 Tbsp chopped fresh cilantro (optional)

Per piece (based on 12 slices):

Calories	180
Total fat	3 g
saturated fat	1.2 g
monounsaturated fat	0.9 g
polyunsaturated fat	0.5 g
Protein	12.3 g
Carbohydrates	25 g
Cholesterol	21 mg
Fiber	2.1 g
Calories from fat	15%

1   Preheat oven to 350°F.

2   In a small bowl, toss the chicken with ¼ cup of the barbecue sauce. Spread the unbaked pizza crusts with the remaining sauce; top with the chicken mixture, cheese, and green onion.

3   Bake for 15–20 minutes or until the cheese melts and crust is golden. If you like, sprinkle with cilantro.

Makes 2 pizzas.

OTHER PIZZA TOPPING IDEAS:

- Caramelized onions, chopped kalamata olives, and crumbled feta

- Slices of fresh ripe tomato, sliced fresh basil, and sliced buffalo mozzarella (Pizza Margherita)

- Roasted vegetables with goat cheese

- Potatoes roasted with lemon, rosemary and olive oil, wilted spinach, artichoke hearts, and goat cheese or feta

- Roasted Garlic & White Bean Spread (page 72), tomatoes, and freshly grated Parmesan cheese

- Basil pesto, shrimp, sun-dried tomatoes, and crumbled feta

Food on a Stick

Who doesn't love food served on a stick?
Corn dogs, Popsicles, Fudgsicles, and caramel
apples all evoke fond childhood memories.
Threading your food onto a stick is a great
way to enforce portion control too—you can
actually count how many skewers you've
gone through!

Poking a skewer through any kind of food
immediately fancies it up, so food on a stick
is perfect for parties. And with no utensils, no
one wonders how to serve themselves. Most
of these recipes can be made in advance
and refrigerated or frozen until you're ready
to grill or broil them—a bonus if you're
expecting company and a lifesaver if you
don't have extra time yourself. (Who does?)
But don't wait for a party—food on a stick is
great any day. Satay became one of my staple
meals while I was writing this book because I
always had a stash in the freezer.

Maple-Rosemary Pork Tenderloin Satay

Pork tenderloin is the best cut of pork for satay; not only is it the leanest and most tender cut, but its shape is conducive to cutting into strips as well. I like to buy bigger packages of pork tenderloin, which are cheaper, and cut a few into strips as soon as I unpack them and freeze in marinade, which acts as insulation against freezer burn.

two 1 lb pork tenderloins

Marinade

¼ cup maple syrup

3 Tbsp lemon juice

3 Tbsp soy sauce

2 Tbsp grainy Dijon (or any mustard you like)

2 Tbsp chopped fresh rosemary

Per satay:

Calories	42
Total fat	0.8 g
saturated fat	0.3 g
monounsaturated fat	0.4 g
polyunsaturated fat	0.1 g
Protein	7.3 g
Carbohydrates	1 g
Cholesterol	17.8 mg
Fiber	0 g
Calories from fat	18%

1 Cut the pork tenderloin in half width-wise, then lengthwise into even strips. Put them into a bowl or Ziploc bag along with the ingredients for the marinade; knead the bag a bit to blend everything, then refrigerate for at least an hour or for up to 24 hours, or freeze for up to 4 months.

2 When you're ready to cook them, soak bamboo skewers in water for about 10 minutes to prevent them from burning, then thread the pork strips onto the skewers, winding them back and forth in an S shape. Grill or broil for a couple minutes per side (depending on the thickness of the pork), just until done. Serve hot, warm, or at room temperature, preferably with peanut sauce (page 65).

Makes about 2½ dozen satay.

Chicken or Pork Satay

Satay are great for a party, a picnic (gather up a satay "bouquet" and wrap the meat ends in foil to transport, along with a tub of peanut sauce), or even dinner, served with veg and some grains. They are also perfect to make ahead and even freeze; the longer they marinate, the more flavorful they'll be, and when frozen the marinade acts as a sort of insulation against freezer burn. Put the frozen bag in a bowl of warm water to thaw them quickly.

1½ lb skinless, boneless chicken breasts or pork tenderloin (1–2), cut into strips

Marinade #1

¼ cup soy sauce

¼ cup orange, lemon, or lime juice

1 Tbsp honey or brown sugar

1 tsp sesame oil (optional)

2 garlic cloves, crushed

1 Tbsp grated fresh ginger

1–2 tsp curry paste or powder

1 green onion, finely chopped (optional)

Marinade #2

½ cup plain yogurt or buttermilk

1 small onion, peeled and grated

3 garlic cloves, crushed

1 Tbsp grated fresh ginger

1 Tbsp soy sauce

1 Tbsp honey or brown sugar

1 Tbsp curry powder

½ tsp cumin

1   Cut the chicken lengthwise into fairly uniform strips (or cut pork tenderloin in half crosswise and then lengthwise into strips) and place in a bowl or Ziploc bag. Combine all the marinade ingredients and pour over the meat; toss well or squish the bag to coat and refrigerate for at least an hour or overnight, or freeze for up to 4 months.

2   When you're ready to cook them, soak some bamboo skewers in water for about 10 minutes to prevent them from burning. Thread the chicken or pork strips onto the skewers, winding them back and forth in an S shape, and grill or broil for a few minutes on each side, until just cooked through. Serve warm, at room temperature, or cold with peanut sauce (page 65) for dipping.

Makes about 20 satay.

Per chicken satay with marinade #1 / #2:

Calories	49 / 46
Total fat	1.3 g / 0.7 g
saturated fat	0.3 g / 0.2 g
monounsaturated fat	0.4 g / 0.2 g
polyunsaturated fat	0.4 g / 0.1 g
Protein	7.7 g / 8 g
Carbohydrates	1.4 g / 1.5 g
Cholesterol	19.7 mg / 20 mg
Fiber	0 g / 0.1 g
Calories from fat	24% / 14%

Teriyaki Beef Sticks

You can often find packages of "stir-fry" beef at the grocery store that has already been cut into strips. Sometimes when I get them home from the grocery store, I pop the beef into a freezer bag, pour over the marinade, and freeze it so I always have something easy on hand for company or just myself.

1 lb lean boneless top round or grilling steak, cut into strips

¼ cup soy sauce

¼ cup honey or brown sugar

2 garlic cloves, crushed

2 Tbsp grated fresh ginger

1 Tbsp lime or lemon juice

Per skewer:

Calories	45
Total fat	1.5 g
saturated fat	0.5 g
monounsaturated fat	0.6 g
polyunsaturated fat	0.1 g
Protein	5.3 g
Carbohydrates	2.5 g
Cholesterol	15.1 mg
Fiber	0 g
Calories from fat	30%

1 Combine soy sauce, honey, garlic, ginger, and lime juice and pour over the beef; stir to coat well and refrigerate for a few hours or overnight.

2 Thread beef onto bamboo skewers that have been soaked in water for at least 10 minutes. Grill or pan-fry for a few minutes on each side, brushing with remaining marinade, until just cooked through.

3 Serve plain or with peanut sauce (page 65) for dipping.

Makes about 1½ dozen skewers.

Jerk Chicken Skewers

Although the ingredient list is long, these are a snap to put together. If you want to prep them in advance, let them marinate for a day or two, or freeze the chicken in its marinade for up to three months; thaw before threading onto skewers and grilling.

1½ lb skinless, boneless chicken breast, pork tenderloin, or beef

4 green onions, chopped

2 garlic cloves, crushed

1 jalapeño or small hot red pepper, seeded and chopped

2 Tbsp orange, lemon, or lime juice

2 Tbsp soy sauce

1 Tbsp canola or olive oil

½ tsp allspice

½ tsp thyme

½ tsp curry powder

¼ tsp cinnamon

¼ tsp ground ginger

¼ tsp nutmeg

¼ tsp salt

¼ tsp freshly ground black pepper

1 Combine everything but the chicken in the bowl of a food processor or blender and whiz until well blended and relatively smooth. Cut the chicken into strips and put them in a bowl or Ziploc baggie; pour the marinade over and stir to coat well. Refrigerate for at least an hour or leave it overnight.

2 When you're ready to cook them, soak your bamboo skewers in water for about 10 minutes to prevent them from burning. Thread the chicken strips onto the skewers, winding them back and forth in an S shape. Grill or broil for a few minutes per side, just until cooked through. Serve warm or at room temperature.

Makes about 20 skewers.

Per skewer:

Calories	44
Total fat	1 g
saturated fat	0.2 g
monounsaturated fat	0.3 g
polyunsaturated fat	0.2 g
Protein	7.7 g
Carbohydrates	0.6 g
Cholesterol	19.7 mg
Fiber	0.1 g
Calories from fat	21%

Honey, Ginger & Sesame Salmon Sticks

To me, these are like candy-on-a-stick; I'd eat the whole lot if no one was around to fight me for them. Salmon is a fatty fish, rich in omega-3 fatty acids, which fight heart disease by lowering triglyceride levels and may have a protective effect against some forms of cancer.

1½ lb salmon fillet

½ cup honey or maple syrup

¼ cup soy sauce

2 Tbsp lime or lemon juice

1 Tbsp finely grated fresh ginger

sesame seeds, toasted, for sprinkling

Per stick:

Calories	80
Total fat	2.7 g
saturated fat	0.6 g
monounsaturated fat	1 g
polyunsaturated fat	1 g
Protein	9.5 g
Carbohydrates	4.9 g
Cholesterol	24.6 mg
Fiber	0 g
Calories from fat	30%

1 Cut salmon into big bite-sized pieces. Combine the honey, soy sauce, and lime juice in a bowl or large Ziploc bag. Add the salmon and stir or shake to coat well. Cover (or seal) and refrigerate for 24 hours, or at least an hour if that's all you have time for.

2 When you're ready to cook them, thread each piece of salmon onto a bamboo skewer that has been soaked in water for at least 10 minutes. Grill over high heat for a couple minutes per side, until just cooked through, or broil for 3–4 minutes. Don't overcook them or the salmon will dry out.

3 Place the sesame seeds in a shallow dish and dip one side of each skewer in the seeds to coat, or sprinkle them overtop. Serve immediately.

Makes about 1½ dozen salmon sticks.

DUKKAH SALMON STICKS (PICTURED)
Don't marinate the salmon at all, but cube, brush with a little oil, and cook it on skewers as directed. Instead of sesame seeds, dip each piece into a shallow dish of Dukkah (page 67).

HONEY-MUSTARD SALMON STICKS
Add 1 Tbsp grainy Dijon mustard to the marinade mixture instead of the ginger.

Greek Lamb Kebabs

This meat-on-a-stick is essentially a Greek-style meatball mixture made with ground lamb instead of beef (although you could use beef or much leaner bison if you like), which is squished into a longish meatball around the end of a bamboo skewer. Alternatively, you could shape the mixture into meatballs; either version is fantastic dipped in garlicky tzatziki or hummus (see page 73 and 68 for recipes), or stuffed into pitas with chopped purple onion, tomato, lettuce, and tzatziki.

1 lb ground lamb, or lean ground beef or bison (or half and half)

1 small onion, peeled and grated

½ cup soft breadcrumbs (about 1 slice of bread) or couscous

½ cup crumbled feta (optional)

4 garlic cloves, crushed

1 large egg

2–4 Tbsp currants or chopped raisins

1 Tbsp grated fresh ginger

1 tsp cumin

¼ tsp ground cinnamon

¼ tsp salt

olive or canola oil, for brushing

Per kebab:

Calories	88
Total fat	3.2 g
saturated fat	1 g
monounsaturated fat	1.4 g
polyunsaturated fat	0.4 g
Protein	9.1 g
Carbohydrates	5.4 g
Cholesterol	43 mg
Fiber	0.5 g
Calories from fat	33%

1 Preheat oven to 400°F.

2 Soak some bamboo skewers in water for at least 10 minutes to prevent them from burning when you cook the kebabs.

3 Combine all the ingredients in a large bowl. Shape handfuls of the meat mixture into flattened sausages about 3 inches long around the ends of the skewers. Place on a rimmed baking sheet, brush with olive oil, and roast, turning often, until cooked through.

Makes 12 kebabs.

YOGURT MINT SAUCE

Stir ¼ cup chopped fresh mint, a crushed clove of garlic, and a tablespoon each of olive oil and lemon juice into a cup of good-quality plain yogurt. Season with salt and pepper.

GREEK MEATBALLS

Shape mixture into balls and place ½ inch apart on a baking pan or rimmed baking sheet. Bake for 15–20 minutes, until cooked through. (Or cook them in a drizzle of oil in a frying pan.) Serve warm or cold with tzatziki or yogurt mint sauce for dipping, or tuck into half a mini pita pocket with tzatziki and a few spring greens.

Vietnamese Pork Meatballs

If you can get your hands on those little grassy bamboo serving picks, they look so great with these. If you want to prep them in advance, freeze the raw meatballs on a baking sheet, and then transfer to a freezer bag to store for up to three months. Place the frozen balls on a baking sheet and pop them in the oven whenever you're ready for them; no need to thaw them first, they'll just take a little longer to cook. They also make a great noodle bowl simmered in stock with noodles and veg.

1 lb lean ground pork, turkey, or chicken, or a combination

1 stalk lemongrass

¼ cup fresh cilantro

1–2 small red chilies or a squirt of chili paste or sambal oelek

4 garlic cloves, crushed

1 Tbsp packed brown sugar

1 Tbsp fish sauce (optional)

1 tsp sesame oil

1 tsp Thai curry paste

1 tsp soy sauce

Per meatball:

Calories	29
Total fat	0.7 g
saturated fat	0.2 g
monounsaturated fat	0.3 g
polyunsaturated fat	0.1 g
Protein	4.6 g
Carbohydrates	0.9 g
Cholesterol	11.2 mg
Fiber	0 g
Calories from fat	22%

1   Preheat oven to 350°F.

2   Remove the tough outer leaves of the lemongrass and chop the tender inner leaves finely. Finely chop the cilantro and chilies as well, removing the stems from the cilantro and seeds from the chilies, unless you want extra heat. Combine all the ingredients in a large bowl, mixing everything well with your hands.

3   Shape the mixture into balls and place about an inch apart on a rimmed baking sheet. Bake for 15–20 minutes, until cooked through. Alternately, you can heat a little sesame or canola oil in a nonstick sauté pan and cook the meatballs over medium heat for 5–10 minutes. I like to flatten them a little with my hand so you get more of the crunchy exterior on each one. Skewer each one with a small bamboo pick or skewer. Serve warm, plain or with peanut sauce (page 65) for dipping.

Makes about 2 dozen meatballs.

Cocktail Meatballs

My love for these meatballs simmered in ketchup and grape jelly is evidence that I'm not a fancy chef. (I am, however, the best eater I know.) This is an old recipe my aunt used to make—if you like sticky, sweet, meaty things and haven't tried some version of cocktail meatballs yet, you must. If you're pressed for time, any of these sauces can be used with lean frozen meatballs.

Meatballs

½ lb each lean ground beef and ground chicken or turkey, or 1 lb ground bison

1 small onion, grated

1 egg white

1 slice bread, processed into crumbs, or ¼ cup cracker crumbs or quick oats

salt, pepper, and garlic powder to taste

Sauce

1 cup bottled chili sauce or ketchup, or half chili sauce and half ketchup

1 cup grape jelly

2 Tbsp lemon juice

Per meatball:

Calories	60
Total fat	1.7 g
saturated fat	0.6 g
monounsaturated fat	0.7 g
polyunsaturated fat	0.1 g
Protein	4.5 g
Carbohydrates	6.7 g
Cholesterol	10.8 mg
Fiber	0.4 g
Calories from fat	26%

1 Preheat oven to 350°F.

2 To prepare the meatballs, combine beef, chicken, onion, egg white, breadcrumbs, salt and pepper, and garlic powder in a medium bowl.

3 Shape the mixture into small balls and place on a baking sheet. Bake for about 20 minutes, until cooked through.

4 For the sauce, combine the ketchup, jelly, and lemon juice in a medium saucepan. Cook over medium heat, stirring often, until bubbly and the jelly has melted. Drop the meatballs into the sauce and simmer for 5 minutes, until heated through.

5 Serve in a chafing dish with toothpicks or in a fondue pot with fondue forks.

Makes about 2 dozen meatballs.

COCKTAIL SAUSAGES

Instead of making the meatballs, cook and slice a few lean chicken or turkey sausages and drop them into the sauce. Simmer until heated through.

SPICY JELLY MEATBALLS

Melt 1 cup peach, apricot, or seedless raspberry jelly or jam with ¼ cup mustard and 1 Tbsp horseradish. Add meatballs or sausage and stir to coat and heat through.

Good Things in Small Packages

Wrapping up food in little packages makes it somehow more festive and special, even when it requires hardly any effort to prepare. The thrill of having something hiding inside, even if it's just cheesy filling, is not lost on adults.

Recipes with long instructions may seem daunting, but they are all a snap to make, even when they do require a little extra effort. It's a shame that cooking is so often portrayed as a chore; I find it to be a creative outlet and one of the most gratifying and therapeutic ways to spend time. All cooks need eaters; in the end, the fact that homemade food is celebratory, comforting, nourishing, and makes people happy is the best reward there is.

Curried Coconut-Mango Chicken in Wonton Cups

Coconut milk is astonishingly high in fat and calories—light coconut milk is a much better choice, and if you want to boost the coconut flavor even further, you can add a drop or two of coconut extract. These cups make great use of leftover roast chicken or turkey.

24 wonton wrappers (plus extra, if you have enough filling for more)

a drizzle of canola or olive oil

1 small onion, finely chopped

2 garlic cloves, crushed

1 Tbsp grated fresh ginger

2 cups chopped cooked chicken or turkey

1 Tbsp curry paste (or to taste)

½ cup light coconut milk or evaporated 2% milk

⅓ cup mango or peach chutney

juice of ½ a lime (about 1 Tbsp)

salt to taste

chopped fresh cilantro (optional)

1 Preheat the oven to 350°F.

2 To make the wonton cups, press fresh wonton wrappers into mini muffin cups, pressing any folds firmly to the sides, and bake for 5–10 minutes, until golden. Set aside to cool.

3 To make the filling, heat about a teaspoon of oil in a frying pan and sauté the onion for about 5 minutes, or until soft. Add the garlic and ginger and cook for another minute. Add the chicken, curry paste, coconut milk, chutney, lime juice, and salt. Cook, stirring often, until bubbly and thickened. Cool slightly or chill before spooning into wonton cups. If you like, sprinkle with cilantro.

Makes 2 dozen cups.

Per cup:

Calories	69
Total fat	1 g
saturated fat	0.3 g
monounsaturated fat	0.3 g
polyunsaturated fat	0.3 g
Protein	7.1 g
Carbohydrates	7.3 g
Cholesterol	16.8 mg
Fiber	0.1 g
Calories from fat	15%

Samosas

Samosas are little packages, and as such can be made with a variety of wrappers—you can buy low-fat samosa wrappers fresh or frozen in ethnic grocery stores, make your own empanada dough, or use phyllo pastry.

A wonderful Indian cook, Tahera Rawji, taught me the easy, cheater's way to make samosa filling—using frozen hash browns! But feel free to boil, peel, and chop potatoes to use in place of the hash browns if you like. Some people like to add a finely chopped jalapeño pepper to the filling too.

Filling

1 Tbsp canola oil

1 onion, finely chopped

3 garlic cloves, crushed

1 Tbsp grated fresh ginger

1 tsp curry powder (optional)

½ tsp ground cumin

¼ tsp ground coriander

¼ tsp turmeric

¼ tsp chili powder

3 cups frozen hash browns, thawed

½–1 cup frozen peas, thawed

1 tsp salt

1 Tbsp lemon juice

1 Tbsp chopped fresh cilantro

½ tsp garam masala

1 pkg phyllo pastry, thawed (you'll need 12–16 sheets)

2 Tbsp butter, melted

2 Tbsp canola or olive oil

1 To prepare the filling, heat the oil over medium heat in a large pan and sauté the onion for about 5 minutes, until soft. Add the garlic, ginger, curry powder (if you like), cumin, coriander, turmeric, and chili powder; cook for a minute, then add the hash browns, peas, salt, and lemon juice. Cook, stirring, for a few minutes, then remove from the heat. Stir in the cilantro and garam masala. Set aside to cool slightly.

2 Preheat oven to 375°F.

3 Take 2 sheets of phyllo and stack them on a clean work surface; cover the rest with a tea towel so they don't dry out. Combine the butter and oil in a small dish and brush the phyllo very lightly with it.

4 Cut the sheet in half lengthwise and then again into quarters so you have 4 long strips. Place a spoonful of filling at one end of each strip and fold the corner over it diagonally. Continue folding the strip as if you were folding a flag, maintaining the triangle shape.

5 Repeat with the remaining phyllo and filling, placing the packets seam side down on a baking sheet. (They can be prepared up to this point and frozen in a single layer and then transferred to a plastic bag. Pop them out of the freezer and bake them frozen.) If there is any butter and oil left, use it to brush the

tops of the triangles, or spray them with some nonstick spray. Bake for 20–25 minutes, until golden.

6   Serve warm with mango chutney.

Makes about 2 dozen samosas.

SPINACH & POTATO SAMOSAS
Replace the frozen peas with a few handfuls of fresh spinach, chopped. Sauté a minced jalapeño pepper along with the garlic and other spices as well.

Per samosa:

Calories	82
Total fat	3.3 g
saturated fat	0.8 g
monounsaturated fat	1.4 g
polyunsaturated fat	0.9 g
Protein	1.7 g
Carbohydrates	11.6 g
Cholesterol	2.6 mg
Fiber	0.7 g
Calories from fat	36%

Vietnamese Rice Paper Rolls

Also called "summer rolls," rice paper rolls are wonderful to learn how to make. They're cheap, portable, perfect party food, and very low in fat and calories. Stuff them with anything you like—thinly sliced red pepper, pea pods, lettuce, crabmeat, blanched asparagus, bean sprouts, chives, jicama, and mango are all delicious. They are fantastic made with shreds of leftover cooked chicken or pork in place of the shrimp, or leave out the meat altogether for vegetarian rolls. All the measurements are approximate—you just need enough to stuff.

15 small to medium rice-paper wrappers

Filling

a handful (about 4 oz) of thin rice vermicelli noodles

1 large carrot, peeled and shredded

1 Tbsp rice vinegar or lime juice

15 cooked shrimp, peeled and deveined

half a cucumber, peeled if necessary and cut into thin sticks

small handful fresh cilantro, mint, or Thai basil leaves, torn up or left whole

¼ cup chopped peanuts or cashews (optional)

Per roll:

Calories	75
Total fat	0.3 g
saturated fat	0.1 g
monounsaturated fat	0.1 g
polyunsaturated fat	0.1 g
Protein	3.6 g
Carbohydrates	14.1 g
Cholesterol	25.3 mg
Fiber	0.2 g
Calories from fat	40%

1   To prepare the filling, place the noodles in a bowl of boiling water and let stand for about 3 minutes (or as the package directs) to soften. Drain well and place in a medium bowl. Add carrot and rice vinegar and toss to combine. Cut the shrimp lengthwise in half.

2   To assemble the rolls, fill a shallow dish (I use a pie plate) with hot water and lay a clean tea towel over your work surface. Soak one rice paper round at a time in the water for about 10 seconds, until it's pliable, and lay it on the tea towel. Pat the surface with the edges of the towel to absorb any excess water. Place 2 shrimp halves (cut side up so you can see the pink through the wrapper), a stick of cucumber and some noodles down the middle of the round. Sprinkle with cilantro and peanuts (if using). Fold over one long side to cover, then fold up both ends. Roll the whole thing up as tightly as you can without tearing the wrapper.

3   Serve with bottled peanut sauce (or make some using the recipe on page 65) or the dipping sauce below.

Makes 15 rolls.

GINGER-MANGO DIPPING SAUCE
Combine ½ cup mango chutney, 2 Tbsp water, 2 Tbsp rice wine vinegar, the juice of 1 lime, and a bit of grated fresh ginger.

Hoisin Pork Lettuce Wraps

Lettuce wraps were in fashion far before Dr. Atkins encouraged us to forgo bread in favor of greens as a sandwich casing. This recipe is simple to make and very stylish to serve on a platter with romaine lettuce leaves; your friends scoop filling onto a leaf, wrap, and eat. Lettuce wraps are substantial enough to make a meal, and perfect to serve at a party or put out on the Scrabble table.

1 Tbsp canola or sesame oil (or some of each)

one 1 lb pork tenderloin or 1 lb skinless, boneless chicken or turkey breast, chopped or cut into small strips

2 garlic cloves, crushed

1 Tbsp grated fresh ginger

2 cups fresh mushrooms, chopped (any kind, or a combination)

1 small red pepper, seeded and finely chopped

¼ cup bottled hoisin sauce, or to taste

½ can water chestnuts, drained and chopped (optional)

salt and pepper to taste

2 green onions, chopped

2 romaine lettuce hearts (the outer leaves tend to be too large)

1 Heat the oil in a large frying pan set over medium-high heat and sauté the pork for a few minutes, until opaque. Add the garlic and ginger and cook for another minute. Add the mushrooms and red pepper and cook until they release their moisture, then start to brown. Add the hoisin sauce and toss to coat and heat through; add the water chestnuts, salt and pepper, and green onions. Remove from heat and set aside.

2 Wash the lettuce well, spin it dry, and separate into leaves, setting aside any really large ones for another use. Transfer the pork mixture to a bowl and arrange on a platter with lettuce leaves around it. To eat, pile some of the pork mixture onto a lettuce leaf, wrap it up, and eat it like a burrito.

Makes about 16 wraps.

CURRIED TUNA LETTUCE WRAPS
Stir together a drained can of tuna, 1 Tbsp lemon juice, a finely chopped rib of celery, ¼ cup low-fat mayonnaise, 1 tsp curry powder, 1 cup halved seedless grapes, and salt and pepper to taste. Serve in place of the hoisin pork mixture.

Per wrap:

Calories	55
Total fat	1.6 g
saturated fat	0.3 g
monounsaturated fat	0.8 g
polyunsaturated fat	0.4 g
Protein	7.6 g
Carbohydrates	2.4 g
Cholesterol	16.7 mg
Fiber	0.5 g
Calories from fat	27%

Spanikopita (Spinach & Feta) Triangles

Phyllo is the Greek word for "leaf" and refers to thinner-than-paper pastry sheets made of flour and water. Phyllo pastry on its own contains almost no fat but can become very high in fat and calories when each layer is slathered with butter. Many low-fat recipes call for nonstick spray between each layer, but they often contain additives and don't have much flavor. I prefer to brush every second layer sparingly with butter or oil instead. If you want to add extra crunch, sprinkle dry breadcrumbs, finely chopped nuts, or grated Parmesan cheese between the layers.

1 pkg phyllo pastry, thawed (you'll need 12–16 sheets)

¼ cup melted butter or canola or olive oil, or half of each

Filling

1 tsp canola oil

1 medium onion, finely chopped

2 garlic cloves, crushed

one 10 oz pkg frozen chopped spinach, thawed and drained

1 cup (about 4 oz) crumbled feta cheese

1 large egg

salt and pepper to taste

Per triangle:

Calories	69
Total fat	4 g
saturated fat	2.1 g
monounsaturated fat	1.1 g
polyunsaturated fat	0.5 g
Protein	2.1 g
Carbohydrates	6.5 g
Cholesterol	19 mg
Fiber	0.5 g
Calories from fat	51%

1 To prepare the filling, heat the oil in a medium frying pan and sauté the onion and garlic over medium heat, until soft. Add spinach and cook until moisture has evaporated. Transfer to a bowl and cool slightly. Stir in the feta, egg, and salt and pepper.

2 Preheat oven to 375°F.

3 Take 2 sheets of phyllo and stack them on a clean work surface; cover the rest with a tea towel so they don't dry out. Brush the phyllo very lightly with butter.

4 Cut the sheet into 4 long strips. Place a spoonful of filling at one end of each strip and fold the corner over it diagonally. Continue folding the strip, maintaining a triangle shape.

5 Repeat with the remaining phyllo and filling, placing the packets seam side down on a baking sheet. (They can be prepared up to this point and frozen in a single layer and then transferred to a plastic bag. Pop them out of the freezer and bake them frozen.)

6 If there is any butter left, use it to brush the tops of the triangles, or spray them with some nonstick spray. Bake for 15–20 minutes, until golden.

Makes 2 dozen triangles.

Three-Cheese Caramelized Onion, Spinach & Mushroom Calzone

A calzone is just a folded-in-half pizza, like a real pizza pocket. They can be filled with anything you'd use to top a pizza. You can freeze them unbaked, then bake them from frozen or take pre-baked frozen calzone to work, and by lunchtime they'll be thawed enough to pop in the microwave and warm up.

1 batch pizza dough (page 115)

1 tsp–1 Tbsp canola oil

1 onion, cut in half and thinly sliced

1 lean Italian sausage, casing removed

2 cups sliced mushrooms

½ red bell pepper, finely chopped

one 10 oz pkg frozen chopped spinach, thawed, and water squeezed out

2 garlic cloves, crushed

1 cup part-skim ricotta cheese

1 large egg

salt and pepper to taste

½ cup grated part-skim mozzarella cheese

¼ cup grated Parmesan cheese

Per calzone:

Calories	545
Total fat	12.7 g
saturated fat	5.7 g
monounsaturated fat	4.2 g
polyunsaturated fat	1.6 g
Protein	26.1 g
Carbohydrates	81.6 g
Cholesterol	81.8 mg
Fiber	6.7 g
Calories from fat	21%

1   Preheat oven to 400°F.

2   In a large nonstick frying pan, heat the oil over medium-high heat and sauté the onions for about 10 minutes, until golden; add the sausage and cook until it is no longer pink. Transfer to a large bowl and set aside.

3   In the same frying pan, sauté the mushrooms and red pepper for about 5 minutes. Add the spinach and garlic; cook until there is no more moisture in the pan. Set aside to cool slightly.

4   Add the ricotta, egg, salt and pepper, spinach mixture, mozzarella, and Parmesan to the sausage and stir well.

5   Divide the pizza dough into 4 balls and roll each out into a 7- to 8-inch circle. Divide the filling between the circles, leaving a ½-inch border. Fold the dough over the filling and press together to seal. Crimp the edge with your fingers or a fork. Transfer to a baking sheet that has been sprayed with nonstick spray, and score the dough. Brush the tops with a little beaten egg if you like.

6   Bake for 10 minutes, and then reduce the oven temperature to 350°F and bake for another 20 minutes, until golden. Let them cool for about 10 minutes before serving.

Makes 4 calzone.

Stromboli

A stromboli is a rolled-up pizzalike sandwich you can hold in your hand. It's not as messy as a calzone, having no tomato sauce, but the roasted peppers make up for it. Any kind of cheese, intensely flavored sliced meats, or even leftover roasted vegetables would go well in a stromboli. It's a meal in itself, or you could slice them on a slight diagonal into 1-inch pieces and serve them as finger food at parties.

1 batch pizza dough (page 115)

¼ cup grated Parmesan cheese

12 slices (about 4 oz) black forest or honey ham or deli roast turkey

12 slices (about 5 oz) thinly sliced provolone, Edam, or mozzarella cheese

1–2 roasted red peppers (page 78), cut into strips

1 egg, lightly beaten

Per stromboli:

Calories	348
Total fat	8.5 g
saturated fat	4.1 g
monounsaturated fat	2.8 g
polyunsaturated fat	0.8 g
Protein	18.9 g
Carbohydrates	47.8 g
Cholesterol	62 mg
Fiber	2.5 g
Calories from fat	22%

1 Preheat oven to 400°F.

2 Divide the dough into 6 pieces and roll each into an 8-inch circle on a lightly floured surface. Sprinkle each piece with Parmesan cheese and layer with ham, provolone, and red peppers.

3 Roll the dough up, folding the ends over and pinching them to seal. Place the rolls on a baking sheet and brush with the beaten egg. Cut a few small vents in each roll to let the steam out.

4 Bake for about 30 minutes, until golden. Let cool slightly before serving.

Makes 6 stromboli.

CARAMELIZED ONION & MUSHROOM STROMBOLI
Sauté a thinly sliced onion in a little oil until golden; add 2 cups of mushrooms and cook until they release their moisture and turn golden as well. Use in place of the ham.

Stuffed Pizza Bites with Saucy Dip

Bite-sized pizza is perfect for little fingers, especially when the filling is enclosed within the crust. These are great to put out on the table when you're watching a movie. Pepperoni is intensely flavored so you don't need to use much, but you could also use ham, mushrooms, chopped roasted red pepper—anything that goes onto pizza works in a pizza bite.

1 can refrigerated breadsticks (such as Pillsbury) or 1 batch pizza dough (page 115)

1 pepperoni stick (about 2 oz) (bison or turkey if you can find it), cut into 24 pieces

three ¼-inch slices (about 3 oz) part-skim mozzarella cheese, cut into cubes

¼ tsp dried Italian seasoning or oregano

1 Tbsp grated Parmesan cheese

1 cup spaghetti or pizza sauce, for dipping

Per piece:

Calories	64
Total fat	2.6 g
saturated fat	0.9 g
monounsaturated fat	0.8 g
polyunsaturated fat	0.1 g
Protein	2.8 g
Carbohydrates	6.9 g
Cholesterol	4.4 mg
Fiber	0.1 g
Calories from fat	38%

1   Preheat oven to 375°F.

2   Unroll the dough and separate it into 8 breadsticks. Cut each one crosswise into thirds to make 24 pieces. Flatten each until it is 1 or 1½ inches wide. (Alternatively, roll out the pizza dough and cut it into 8 strips, then crosswise into thirds.)

3   Place a piece of pepperoni and a square of cheese in the middle of each piece of dough and fold over the ends to enclose them, pressing the edges to seal. Place seam side down on a baking sheet.

4   Sprinkle the bundles with Italian seasoning and Parmesan cheese. Bake for 15–20 minutes, until golden. Serve immediately. Warm the spaghetti sauce and serve alongside for dipping.

Makes 24 bites.

Jalapeño Poppers

The first time I tasted these in a pub they were just this side of awful, and I've been determined to make them the way I think they ought to taste ever since. Although I'm a wimp when it comes to spice levels, I'm a sucker for anything gooily cheesy, and I was pleasantly surprised at how mild the peppers were baked without their seeds and membrane—almost like green bell peppers without the bitterness and with a little more kick.

6 good-sized fresh jalapeño peppers

half of an 8 oz pkg light cream cheese, softened

½ cup grated mozzarella, cheddar, or Monterey Jack cheese

½ tsp ground cumin (optional)

pinch cayenne (optional)

2 large eggs

½ cup all-purpose flour

½ tsp garlic powder

salt and pepper to taste

1–2 cups panko (crunchy Japanese breadcrumbs), or fine dry breadcrumbs

salsa, for dipping (optional)

Per popper:

Calories	87
Total fat	3.6 g
saturated fat	1.7 g
monounsaturated fat	1.2 g
polyunsaturated fat	0.3 g
Protein	4 g
Carbohydrates	9.5 g
Cholesterol	43.2 mg
Fiber	0.5 g
Calories from fat	37%

1   Preheat the oven to 350°F.

2   Wearing rubber gloves, cut the jalapeños in half lengthwise and remove the seeds and membranes.

3   In a small bowl, stir together the cream cheese, mozzarella, cumin, and cayenne if you're using it. Stuff the jalapeño halves with the cheese mixture—they will be overflowing! That's okay. When I do this, I take a bit of cheese in my hand and roll it into a cylinder, then press it into the pepper.

4   Get 3 shallow dishes. In one, beat the eggs with a fork. In another, combine the flour, garlic powder, and salt and pepper. Put the crumbs into a third.

5   One at a time, dredge the jalapeños in flour, then in the beaten egg, and then in the crumbs, pressing to coat well. Place the coated peppers, cut side up, on a baking sheet that has been sprayed with nonstick spray.

6   Bake for about 30 minutes, until golden and bubbly. Serve immediately, with salsa for dipping if you like.

Makes 12 poppers.

Pot Stickers

When I make pot stickers, I make a large batch and freeze half to throw into simmering stock to make fast wonton soup. You can find square or round wonton wrappers fresh or frozen in Asian markets and most grocery stores. If the pre-ground pork you find in the meat department seems too fatty, buy pork tenderloin, chop it, and pulse until finely ground in your food processor.

Filling

1 cup finely chopped bok choy or napa cabbage

¼ tsp salt

½ lb lean ground pork

1 cup thinly sliced mushrooms

2 green onions, finely chopped

1 Tbsp soy sauce

1–2 garlic cloves, crushed

1 tsp grated fresh ginger

½ tsp sugar

1 tsp sesame oil

1 pkg wonton wrappers (about 30)

1 Tbsp canola oil

chicken stock or water

Per pot sticker:

Calories	45
Total fat	1 g
saturated fat	0.2 g
monounsaturated fat	0.4 g
polyunsaturated fat	0.3 g
Protein	3 g
Carbohydrates	5.9 g
Cholesterol	5.2 mg
Fiber	0.4 g
Calories from fat	20%

1 To prepare the filling, toss the cabbage with salt in a medium bowl and let it stand for 5 minutes. Pick it up in your hands and squeeze out the excess liquid, draining it as well as you can. Add the pork, mushrooms, green onions, soy sauce, garlic, ginger, sugar, and sesame oil and mix it all up with your hands.

2 To fill the wontons, place a small spoon-ful of filling in the middle of each wrap-per; moisten the edges with water (just use your finger) and fold over, pressing the edge tightly to seal. Place seam side up on a baking sheet, pressing lightly so that they settle and flatten a bit on the bottom. Cover with a tea towel to pre-vent them from drying out. (Pot stickers can be prepared up to this point, covered with plastic wrap, and refrigerated for up to 24 hours or frozen.)

3 When you're ready to cook the pot stick-ers, heat the canola oil in a large frying pan over medium-high heat. Place half the pot stickers at a time in the frying pan and cook for a minute or two, until deep golden brown on the bottom, shak-ing the pan a few times to keep them from *really* sticking. (If they are sticking, leave them alone for a minute to develop a nice crust on the bottom, then try again.) Don't crowd the pan too much or they will steam rather than brown properly.

4　Pour about ⅓ cup stock or water into the pan. Cover, reduce heat to medium, and cook for about 5 minutes—this will allow them to steam and cook through. Uncover and cook until the bottoms of the pot stickers are very crisp and the liquid has evaporated, about 5–7 more minutes. Repeat with the remaining pot stickers.

Makes 2–2½ dozen pot stickers.

GARLIC-CHILI DIPPING SAUCE

¼ cup soy sauce

2 Tbsp packed brown sugar

2 Tbsp rice vinegar

2 Tbsp lime or lemon juice

1 tsp sesame oil

2 garlic cloves, crushed

1 green onion, chopped

1 tsp chili sauce or sambal oelek

Mix all the ingredients together in a bowl or shake them all up in a jar.

Makes about ¾ cup.

OTHER POT STICKER FILLINGS TO TRY:

GARLICKY SCALLOP
Omit the cabbage and salt. Replace the pork with chopped fresh scallops, and add 3 more cloves of crushed garlic to the mixture.

PEANUT CHICKEN
Fill the wrappers with a mixture of ½ lb ground chicken or turkey, 4 chopped green onions, ¼ cup chopped fresh cilantro, ¼ cup chopped roasted peanuts, 1 egg, 1 tsp grated fresh ginger, and salt and pepper.

ASIAN ASPARAGUS
Finely chop 1 Tbsp minced fresh ginger, 2 garlic cloves, 1 cup chopped, blanched fresh asparagus, 1 can drained water chestnuts, 3 green onions, 1 tsp sesame oil, and 1 tsp soy sauce in a food processor. If you happen to have some, stir in some finely chopped roast duck or chicken.

CRAB
Mix 1 lb crabmeat, 1 egg white, 1 Tbsp rice vinegar, 1 Tbsp grated fresh ginger, 1 tsp sesame oil, and 2 Tbsp chopped fresh cilantro.

PORK & SHRIMP
Combine ¼ lb each ground pork and finely chopped uncooked shrimp, 1 egg white, ¼ cup finely chopped water chestnuts, 1 Tbsp chopped fresh cilantro, 1 tsp grated fresh ginger, and ½ tsp each sugar, salt, and sesame oil.

SHRIMP & SPINACH
Blanch a packed cup of spinach or chard in simmering water for a few seconds, until wilted. Drain well, squeeze out as much moisture as possible, and chop finely. Stir in 1 cup of uncooked, chopped shrimp, ¼ cup finely chopped water chestnuts, 2 finely chopped green onions, 1 tsp sesame oil, 2 tsp grated fresh ginger, 1 tsp sugar, and ½ tsp salt.

Lovin' from the Oven

Home cooks seem to be divided into two camps: bakers and chefs. Some love to bake, and others prefer to cook meals. For me, the act of baking itself is as addictive and satisfying as the end result. Unfortunately home baking is also the ultimate test of self-control, so it's best to only bake when there are other people around to save you from yourself. This is why people who bake also tend to make a lot of friends.

Peanut Butter Power Bars

These are perfect for those days when you need a little ammo in your bag to combat the vending machine. They can be made with any combination of dried fruit, nuts, and seeds you like; the more the merrier!

½ cup packed brown sugar

¼ cup all-natural or light peanut butter

¼ cup 1% milk or soy milk

¼ cup honey or maple syrup

2 Tbsp canola oil

1 tsp vanilla

¾ cup whole wheat, quinoa, or oat flour

¾ cup oats

½ tsp baking soda

¼ tsp cinnamon

pinch salt

½ cup dried fruit, such as raisins, cranberries, and chopped apricots

½ cup chocolate chips

¼ cup sliced almonds

¼ cup sunflower seeds and/or sesame seeds

2 Tbsp ground flax seeds

¼ cup pumpkin seeds

¼ cup shredded coconut (optional)

1   Preheat oven to 350°F.

2   In a large bowl, stir together the brown sugar, peanut butter, milk, honey, oil, and vanilla. Add the flour, oats, baking soda, cinnamon, and salt and stir until almost combined; add the dried fruit, chocolate chips, almonds, sunflower seeds, ground flax seeds, pumpkin seeds, and coconut (if using) and stir just until blended.

3   Spread the batter into a 9- × 13-inch pan that has been sprayed with nonstick spray. The mixture will be sticky—I find it easiest to do this with dampened hands. Bake for 20 minutes, or until pale golden around the edges. Cool in the pan on a wire rack.

Makes 18 bars.

Per bar:

Calories	171
Total fat	7 g
saturated fat	1.5 g
monounsaturated fat	3 g
polyunsaturated fat	2.2 g
Protein	3.5 g
Carbohydrates	26.3 g
Cholesterol	0 mg
Fiber	2.3 g
Calories from fat	34%

Peanut Butter Cookies (the Easiest & Best)

Because they contain only three ingredients, and no flour, these über-simple peanut butter cookies have a shortbread-like consistency and can be stirred together in under a minute. The dough might seem too wet at first; keep stirring and it should firm up. Once it resembles cookie dough, stop stirring, or it could become crumbly and dry.

1½ cups light or all-natural peanut butter

½ cup sugar

½ cup packed brown sugar

1 large egg white

Per cookie:

Calories	110
Total fat	5.6 g
saturated fat	1 g
monounsaturated fat	2.4 g
polyunsaturated fat	1.9 g
Protein	3 g
Carbohydrates	13.7 g
Cholesterol	0 mg
Fiber	0 g
Calories from fat	43%

1. Preheat oven to 350°F.

2. In a large bowl, stir together the peanut butter, sugar, brown sugar, and egg white until well blended.

3. Roll dough into 1½ inch balls and place about 2 inches apart on an ungreased baking sheet. Press down on each cookie once or twice with the back of a fork.

4. Bake for 12–14 minutes, until just barely golden around the edges. Gently transfer to a wire rack to cool.

Makes 2 dozen cookies.

Breakfast Bean Cookies

Packed with protein, fiber, vitamins, and minerals, beans are a great way to sneak nutrition into cookies—puréed, you don't even know they're there! These are substantial and not too sweet, and they have an amazingly tender texture and keep longer than other low-fat cookies. I call them breakfast cookies because they make a perfect mobile mini meal.

2 cups oats (quick or old-fashioned, not instant)

1 cup all-purpose flour

1 tsp baking powder

1 tsp baking soda

½ tsp cinnamon

¼ tsp salt

one 19 oz can white kidney or navy beans, rinsed and drained

¼ cup butter or nonhydrogenated margarine, softened

1 cup packed brown sugar

1 large egg

2 tsp vanilla

½ cup chocolate chips

½ cup raisins or dried cranberries

¼–½ cup chopped walnuts or pecans

2–4 Tbsp ground flax seeds (optional)

Per cookie:

Calories	165
Total fat	4.9 g
saturated fat	2.3 g
monounsaturated fat	1.3 g
polyunsaturated fat	1 g
Protein	3.7 g
Carbohydrates	27.3 g
Cholesterol	14.5 mg
Fiber	2.4 g
Calories from fat	26%

1 Preheat oven to 350°F.

2 Place the oats in the bowl of a food processor and pulse until it resembles coarse flour. Add the flour, baking powder, baking soda, cinnamon, and salt and process until combined. Transfer to a large bowl.

3 Put the beans into the food processor and pulse until roughly puréed. Add butter and process until well blended. Add the brown sugar, egg, and vanilla and pulse until smooth, scraping down the sides of the bowl.

4 Pour the bean mixture into the oat mixture and stir by hand until almost combined; add the chocolate chips, raisins, nuts, and ground flax seeds (if using) and stir just until blended.

5 Drop large spoonfuls of dough onto a baking sheet that has been sprayed with nonstick spray, and flatten each one a little with your hand. (I find this works best if I dampen my hands first.) Bake for 14–16 minutes, until pale golden around the edges but still soft in the middle. Transfer to a wire rack to cool.

Makes 2 dozen cookies.

Hot Soft Pretzels

Like bagels, boiling these pretzels for a minute before baking them gives them a chewy texture. The dough can be rolled into ropes and twisted into any shape, making this a fun project if you have kids around.

1 pkg active dry yeast (or 2½ tsp)

1 Tbsp packed brown sugar

1½ cups warm water (105°F–110°F)

1 tsp salt

2 cups all-purpose flour

2 cups whole wheat flour

extra flour, for dusting work surface

½ tsp baking soda

coarse sea salt or kosher salt for sprinkling

Per pretzel:

Calories	150
Total fat	0.6 g
saturated fat	0.1 g
monounsaturated fat	0.1 g
polyunsaturated fat	0.2 g
Protein	5.1 g
Carbohydrates	31.8 g
Cholesterol	0 mg
Fiber	3.3 g
Calories from fat	4%

OLIVE & GARLIC PRETZELS

Pulse ½ cup kalamata olives, 2 cloves garlic, and, if you like, 1 anchovy fillet in a food processor until finely chopped. Add to the yeast mixture along with the flour.

PIZZA PRETZELS

Instead of sprinkling with salt, brush unbaked pretzels with tomato sauce and sprinkle with grated Parmesan cheese.

1 In a large bowl combine yeast, half the brown sugar, and ½ cup water and let stand 5 minutes until foamy. Add remaining sugar and water and stir well. Add 1 cup of flour and the salt and stir until well blended. Add the remaining flour 1 cup at a time, mixing by hand until incorporated. On a lightly floured surface, knead the dough for 5–7 minutes, until smooth and elastic. Transfer to a bowl, cover with a tea towel, and let stand in a warm place for 40 minutes.

2 Dust your work surface with flour. Divide dough into 12 pieces and roll into long, ½-inch-thick ropes. Shape into pretzels, pressing ends to secure the dough. Cover with a tea towel and let rise on the countertop or on a baking sheet for 20–30 minutes.

3 Preheat oven to 450°F. Bring a large pot of water to a boil and stir in the baking soda. Drop the pretzels into the boiling water a couple at a time and cook for 1 minute, then flip and cook on the other side for a minute. Using a slotted spoon, transfer pretzels to a baking sheet and sprinkle with coarse salt. Bake for 10–12 minutes, until golden.

4 Serve warm, on their own, or drizzled with mustard.

Makes 1 dozen pretzels.

Bagels

Bagels are easy to buy, but almost as easy to make yourself. If you're like me and love to bake, you may even find the process therapeutic! And nothing beats a hot bagel straight from the oven. The problem with store-bought bagels is their size—the ones that are close to the size of your head can weigh in at 500 calories apiece, even though they are low in fat. You can flavor these any way you like by stirring in some grated cheese, caramelized onions, fresh garlic, dried blueberries, toasted nuts, or seeds.

1 Tbsp active dry yeast

1 Tbsp brown sugar

1 Tbsp canola or olive oil

4–5 cups all-purpose flour (or use half all-purpose and half whole wheat)

2 tsp salt

sesame, poppy, or caraway seeds to sprinkle on top (optional)

Per bagel:

Calories	222
Total fat	1.9 g
saturated fat	0.2 g
monounsaturated fat	0.9 g
polyunsaturated fat	0.6 g
Protein	5.8 g
Carbohydrates	44.3 g
Cholesterol	0 mg
Fiber	1.7 g
Calories from fat	8%

1   In a large bowl, stir yeast and brown sugar into 1½ cups lukewarm water until it dissolves; let it stand for 5 minutes until it gets foamy. If it doesn't, the yeast is probably expired—toss it and get some fresh yeast!

2   Stir the oil and 1 cup of the flour into the yeast mixture, then add the salt and enough of the remaining flour to make a soft dough—I usually use about 2½ cups. Turn the dough out onto a lightly floured surface and knead, gently incorporating more flour, until the dough is smooth and elastic. It should take about 10 minutes. Cover with a tea towel and let it rest for about 15 minutes.

3   Divide the dough into 10 pieces. Roll each piece into a rope and then shape it into a circle, pinching the ends together to form bagels. Let them rise for about 20 minutes while you boil a big pot (about 6 quarts/liters) of salted water and preheat the oven to 450°F.

4   When the water comes to a boil, reduce the heat to a simmer and gently place a few bagels at a time into the water. Simmer for 1 minute, then flip them over and cook for another 30 seconds. Remove them with a slotted spoon and place on a wire rack to drain. Once they have all been boiled, place them on a baking sheet that has been sprayed with nonstick spray, and if you like, sprinkle with sesame seeds or whatever toppings you like.

5 Place in the oven, reduce heat to 425°F, and bake for 20 minutes, until golden.

Makes 10 bagels.

CINNAMON-RAISIN BAGELS
Add 1 tsp cinnamon and ½–1 cup raisins along with the second batch of flour.

ONION & GARLIC BAGELS
Sauté 1 minced onion and a few cloves of crushed garlic in 1 tsp oil until tender and golden. Cool and stir into the dough along with the second batch of flour.

CHEESE BAGELS
Add 1 tsp garlic powder and 1 cup grated old cheddar or ½ cup grated Parmesan cheese along with the second batch of flour. Sprinkle the tops of the bagels with a little extra grated cheese before baking.

Focaccia

Focaccia dough is very similar to pizza dough, but in the end it's more like a thick flatbread with less stuff on top. Tear it up to use as a dipper or split and fill it to make a sandwich. When you pat out the dough, you could bake it as a single loaf or cut it with a small round cutter to make mini focaccias, which go very well with any kind of spread or can be used in place of crostini.

1 cup warm water

½ tsp sugar

1½ tsp active dry yeast

2¼–2½ cups all-purpose flour

1 tsp salt

freshly ground black pepper, to taste

1 Tbsp olive oil

Topping

1 Tbsp olive oil

2 garlic cloves, crushed, or 1 Tbsp chopped fresh rosemary or thyme

1 tsp coarse sea salt

Per wedge:

Calories	162
Total fat	3.8 g
saturated fat	0.5 g
monounsaturated fat	2.5 g
polyunsaturated fat	0.4 g
Protein	4 g
Carbohydrates	27.6 g
Cholesterol	0 mg
Fiber	1.3 g
Calories from fat	21%

1 Combine water and sugar in a large bowl; sprinkle with yeast and let stand until foamy. If the yeast doesn't foam, it is either inactive or the water you used was too hot and it killed it. Buy fresh yeast or try again!

2 Stir in 2 cups of the flour, salt, pepper, and olive oil. Knead in enough of the remaining flour until you have a soft, not sticky, dough. Knead for a few minutes, until it's smooth and elastic.

3 Transfer the dough to an oiled bowl (roll the dough in the bowl so it gets coated with oil too), cover with a tea towel, and let it rise in a warm place until doubled in bulk—about 45 minutes. If you want to make this ahead, let it rise in the fridge covered with plastic wrap for 24 hours.

4 Pat the dough into a 9- or 10-inch circle on a baking sheet. Poke holes with your finger all over the top and scatter or drizzle the toppings overtop. Cover loosely with plastic wrap and let rise for about an hour, until doubled. Preheat the oven to 400°F.

5 Bake focaccia for 20–30 minutes, until it's golden and sounds hollow when tapped.

Makes 1 focaccia; serves 8.

CARAMELIZED ONION & PARMESAN FOCACCIA

Toss a thinly sliced onion with olive or canola oil and spread over the unbaked dough. Sprinkle with grated Parmesan cheese and bake as directed, adding a few extra minutes to the baking time.

OLIVE & FETA FOCACCIA

Add ¼ cup chopped kalamata olives to the dough along with the olive oil. Shape and poke the dough all over with your finger to make deep dents; top with ¼ cup crumbled feta and a drizzle of olive oil before baking.

GRAPE FOCACCIA

Instead of drizzling the poked dough with olive oil, scatter with about a cup of small or halved seedless purple grapes and press them into the dough. Sprinkle with some chopped walnuts or fresh rosemary and ¼ cup sugar—coarse sugar is perfect if you can get it—and bake as directed. Or omit the sugar and sprinkle the baked focaccia with icing sugar.

Whole Wheat–Olive Oil Biscuits

These are made healthier with the addition of olive oil and whole wheat flour, but you can use all-purpose flour only, if you like. To flavor the dough, add grated lemon or orange zest, ginger, fresh or dried herbs (such as basil or rosemary), or spices, or stir in a handful of grated cheese, chopped nuts, chocolate, or fresh, frozen, or dried berries.

1 cup all-purpose flour

1 cup whole wheat flour

1 Tbsp sugar (optional)

1 Tbsp baking powder

¼ tsp each baking soda and salt

2 Tbsp butter, chilled and cut into pieces

¼ cup olive or canola oil

¾ cup milk or buttermilk

any additions you like (or none)

Per plain biscuit (based on 8 wedges):

Calories	204
Total fat	10.3 g
saturated fat	2.9 g
monounsaturated fat	5.9 g
polyunsaturated fat	1 g
Protein	4.5 g
Carbohydrates	24.2 g
Cholesterol	8.7 mg
Fiber	2.4 g
Calories from fat	45%

Per plain biscuit (based on 12 rounds):

Calories	136
Total fat	6.9 g
saturated fat	2 g
monounsaturated fat	4 g
polyunsaturated fat	0.6 g
Protein	3 g
Carbohydrates	16.2 g
Cholesterol	5.8 mg
Fiber	1.6 g
Calories from fat	45%

1 Preheat oven to 400°F. Spray a baking sheet with nonstick spray.

2 Put the flours, sugar, baking powder, baking soda, and salt in the bowl of a food processor or into a mixing bowl and pulse or stir until well blended. Add the butter and oil and pulse or stir with a wire whisk or fork until crumbly. If you're using a food processor, transfer the mixture to a medium bowl.

3 Add the milk and stir gently until the dough begins to come together. Add any additions (cheese, raisins, nuts, fruit, etc.) and stir just until combined.

4 For wedge-shaped biscuits, pat the dough into a circle about 1 inch thick on the baking sheet. (If they are sweet and you want a brown, crunchy top, brush them with a little milk and sprinkle with sugar.) Cut the circle into 8 wedges with a knife or pastry cutter and separate them on the sheet so that they are at least an inch apart. For round biscuits, pat the dough about 1 inch thick on a lightly floured surface and cut into rounds with a biscuit cutter, glass rim, or open end of a can, rerolling the scraps only once to get as many biscuits as possible.

5 Bake for 15–20 minutes, until golden. Serve warm. Wrap well and freeze any you don't eat the same day.

Makes 8–12 biscuits.

BERRY, WHOLE WHEAT & WHITE CHOCOLATE DROP SCONES

Increase the milk to 1 cup and stir an egg into it with a fork; stir 1 cup fresh or frozen berries and ½ cup white chocolate chips or chunks into the batter. Drop the batter in large spoonfuls onto the baking sheet to bake.

WHOLE WHEAT & OLIVE OIL CHEESE BISCUITS

Add ¼ cup grated Parmesan cheese to the dry ingredients; omit the sugar. If you like, toss ¼–½ cup grated old cheddar along with the Parmesan.

LEMON-POPPYSEED BISCUITS

Add the finely grated zest of 1 lemon and ¼ cup poppy seeds to the dry ingredients; blend in well before adding the wet ingredients.

MINIATURE CURRANT SCONES

Add ½ cup dried currants to the flour mixture, and stir an egg into the milk before adding it. Pat the dough 1 inch thick and cut into 1½-inch rounds with a small round cookie cutter. Bake until golden.

GINGER SCONES

Add ¼ cup chopped crystallized ginger to the dry ingredients once it's blended; stir an egg and 1 tsp–1 Tbsp grated fresh ginger to the milk.

Cinnamon Sticky Biscuits

I am such a sucker for cinnamon sticky buns, but at about 700 calories and 30+ grams of fat in some bakery cinnamon buns, I can't afford to indulge very often. Because the biscuit dough doesn't require any rising, these can satisfy an immediate craving for freshly baked cinnamon buns. For a phenomenal fruit cobbler, try laying thin slices of these biscuits on top of a dish of peaches or apples tossed with sugar, then bake at 350°F for 20–30 minutes, until golden and bubbly around the edges.

Stickiness

2 Tbsp butter

¼ cup packed brown sugar

1 Tbsp honey, maple syrup, or corn syrup

Biscuits

1 cup all-purpose flour

1 cup whole wheat flour

1 Tbsp baking powder

1 Tbsp sugar

¼ tsp salt

¾ cup milk

¼ cup canola oil

Filling

½ cup packed brown sugar

½ tsp cinnamon

¼ cup raisins and/or chopped pecans (optional)

Per biscuit:

Calories	265
Total fat	9 g
saturated fat	2.2 g
monounsaturated fat	4.4 g
polyunsaturated fat	2 g
Protein	4 g
Carbohydrates	43 g
Cholesterol	7.7 mg
Fiber	2.1 g
Calories from fat	30%

1 Preheat oven to 400°F.

2 For the stickiness, put the butter, brown sugar, and honey in the bottom of an 8- × 8-inch baking pan that has been sprayed with nonstick spray. Put the pan into the oven as it warms up, while you make the biscuits, and when you take it out of the oven to add the biscuits, stir the butter-sugar mixture in the bottom of the pan with a fork until smooth.

3 For the biscuits, combine flours, baking powder, sugar, and salt in a large bowl. Add the milk and canola oil and stir by hand just until you have a soft dough. Do not overmix or they could become tough.

4 For the filling, on a lightly floured surface, pat or roll the dough into a 9- × 14-inch rectangle. Sprinkle with brown sugar, cinnamon, and, if you like, raisins and/or nuts. Starting from a long side, roll jelly-roll style into a log. Cut into 9 biscuits using dental floss or a serrated knife, and place cut side down in 3 rows of 3 in the pan.

5 Bake for 20 minutes, until golden and bubbly. Invert onto a platter while still warm.

Makes 9 biscuits.

APRICOT STICKY BISCUITS

Spray a muffin pan with nonstick spray and divide the brown sugar goo between them, then place a canned apricot half cut side down in each cup. Place the biscuits on top and bake for 20 minutes, until golden.

APPLE PIE ROLLS

Sprinkle the dough with a peeled and finely chopped tart apple or pear along with the brown sugar and cinnamon. Roll and bake as directed.

MINCEMEAT ROLLS

Spread the dough with jarred all-fruit mincemeat instead of sprinkling with brown sugar and nuts; roll and bake as directed.

GARLIC CHEESE ROLLS

Omit the stickiness and filling, and instead spread the rolled dough with a mixture of 1 Tbsp butter, 1 Tbsp canola or olive oil, and 2 crushed cloves of garlic. Sprinkle with ½ cup grated Parmesan or old cheddar cheese; roll, cut, and bake as directed.

Banana Bread

Everyone should be armed with a good banana bread recipe in their repertoire. It makes great peanut butter sandwiches, or try toasting it and spreading with soft cream cheese. To make banana muffins, bake batter in paper-lined muffin tins at 400°F for 20–25 minutes.

¼ cup canola oil, or butter or nonhydrogenated margarine, softened

¾ cup sugar

2–3 mashed very ripe bananas

2 large eggs

⅓ cup plain low-fat yogurt, low-fat sour cream, or buttermilk

2 tsp vanilla

1 cup all-purpose flour

1 cup whole wheat flour

1 tsp baking soda

¼ tsp salt

½ cup chopped walnuts, pecans, raisins, or chocolate chips (optional)

OR

1 cup fresh or frozen (unthawed) blueberries

Per slice:

Calories	153
Total fat	4.4 g
saturated fat	0.6 g
monounsaturated fat	2.3 g
polyunsaturated fat	1.2 g
Protein	3.1 g
Carbohydrates	26.3 g
Cholesterol	27.2 mg
Fiber	1.6 g
Calories from fat	25%

1 Preheat oven to 350°F.

2 In a large bowl, stir the oil or butter and sugar together until well combined—the mixture will have the consistency of wet sand. Add the banana, eggs, yogurt, and vanilla and beat until well blended; don't worry about getting all the lumps of banana out.

3 Add the flours, baking soda, and salt and stir by hand just until combined. If you are adding nuts or other additions, throw them in before the batter is blended.

4 Pour batter into an 8- × 4-inch loaf pan that has been sprayed with nonstick spray. Bake for 1 hour and 10 minutes, until the top is springy to the touch. Cool in the pan on a wire rack.

Makes 1 loaf, with about 16 slices.

CHOCOLATE SWIRL BANANA BREAD
Remove 1 cup of batter and gently stir 2 Tbsp cocoa into it. Alternate big spoonfuls of plain and chocolate batter in the pan and gently run a knife through to create a marbled effect.

LEMON BANANA BREAD
Add the grated zest of 1 lemon to the butter and sugar mixture. Brush the warm loaf with a glaze made of ¼ cup icing sugar and 1 Tbsp lemon juice.

Apple-Muesli Bread

This sturdy, grainy bread is the perfect vehicle for peanut butter or cream cheese but is just as good plain. Use any assortment of dried fruit, nuts, and seeds, or try adding fresh or frozen berries.

1½ cups whole wheat flour

1 cup all-purpose flour

½ cup quick oats

¾ cup sugar

1 Tbsp baking powder

½ tsp salt

1½ cups milk

¼ cup canola oil or melted butter

1 large egg

1 grated apple, peeled or unpeeled

½ cup dried fruit, such as raisins, cranberries, and chopped apricots

½ cup coarsely chopped nuts (pecans, walnuts, almonds, hazelnuts, or a combination)

Per slice:

Calories	212
Total fat	7.1 g
saturated fat	0.9 g
monounsaturated fat	3.8 g
polyunsaturated fat	1.9 g
Protein	4.8 g
Carbohydrates	34.3 g
Cholesterol	15.2 mg
Fiber	2.5 g
Calories from fat	29%

1 Preheat oven to 350°F.

2 In a large bowl combine flours, oats, sugar, baking powder, and salt. In a small bowl, whisk together the milk, oil, and egg.

3 Make a well in the dry ingredients and add the milk mixture along with the apple. Stir a few strokes, then add the dried fruit and nuts and stir just until combined.

4 Spread into a 9- × 5-inch loaf pan that has been sprayed with nonstick spray. If you like, sprinkle another spoonful of oats over the top. Bake for 1 hour, until golden and the top is cracked and springy to the touch. Cool in the pan on a wire rack.

Makes 1 loaf, with about 16 slices.

WHOLE WHEAT & BERRY BREAD
Replace the dried fruit with fresh or frozen berries and add the grated zest of a lemon.

WHOLE WHEAT & NUT BREAD
Omit the apple and dried fruit and increase the nuts to 1 cup.

APPLE-MUESLI MUFFINS
Divide the batter among 12 muffin cups that have been sprayed with nonstick spray or lined with paper liners; bake at 400°F for 20–25 minutes, until golden and springy to the touch.

Zucchini-Walnut Bread

Here's a great way to use up a zucchini surplus at the end of summer. This loaf has a similar texture to carrot cake; if you like, add a grated carrot along with the zucchini as well.

1 cup all-purpose flour

1 cup whole wheat flour

¾ cup sugar

1 Tbsp baking powder

½ tsp baking soda

½ tsp cinnamon (optional)

¼ tsp salt

¾ cup milk

¼ cup canola oil

2 large eggs

grated zest of 1 lemon (optional)

2 cups grated unpeeled zucchini (about 1 medium zucchini)

½ cup chopped walnuts or pecans

Per slice:

Calories	161
Total fat	6.5 g
saturated fat	0.7 g
monounsaturated fat	2.8 g
polyunsaturated fat	2.6 g
Protein	4 g
Carbohydrates	22.6 g
Cholesterol	27.2 mg
Fiber	1.5 g
Calories from fat	36%

1 Preheat oven to 350°F.

2 In a large bowl combine the flours, sugar, baking powder, baking soda, cinnamon, and salt.

3 In a small bowl, whisk together the milk, oil, eggs, and lemon zest (if using) and add to the flour mixture along with the grated zucchini and walnuts. Stir by hand just until combined. Don't worry about getting all the lumps out.

4 Pour into an 8- × 4-inch loaf pan that has been sprayed with nonstick spray, and bake for 1 hour, until golden and springy to the touch. Cool in the pan on a wire rack.

Makes 1 loaf, with about 16 slices.

ZUCCHINI-WALNUT MUFFINS
Divide the batter among 12 muffin cups that have been sprayed with nonstick spray or lined with paper liners; bake at 400°F for 20–25 minutes, until golden and springy to the touch.

Pumpkin Bread with Cranberries & Pecans

I always find myself baking with pumpkin in the fall, when its spicy warmth and aroma seems the most gratifyingly cozy and old-fashioned. Pumpkin, especially the canned variety, adds moisture and flavor to any loaf and is an excellent source of nutrients, particularly beta-carotene.

¼ cup butter or nonhydrogenated margarine, softened

1 cup sugar

1 large egg

one 14 oz can pumpkin purée

1 tsp vanilla

2 cups all-purpose flour

2 tsp cinnamon

1 tsp baking powder

½ tsp baking soda

½ tsp salt

¾ cup buttermilk

½ cup dried cranberries, or 1 cup fresh

½ cup chopped pecans

Per slice:

Calories	174
Total fat	5.8 g
saturated fat	2.2 g
monounsaturated fat	2.4 g
polyunsaturated fat	0.8 g
Protein	2.8 g
Carbohydrates	28.2 g
Cholesterol	21.6 mg
Fiber	1.2 g
Calories from fat	30%

1 Preheat oven to 350°F.

2 In a medium bowl, beat butter and sugar until well blended—it will have the consistency of wet sand. Add the egg, pumpkin, and vanilla and beat until smooth.

3 In another bowl stir together the flour, cinnamon, baking powder, baking soda, and salt. Add about a third to the butter mixture and stir by hand just until combined. Add half the buttermilk in the same manner, then another third of the flour, the remaining buttermilk, and remaining flour along with the cranberries and pecans.

4 Pour the batter into an 8- × 4-inch or 9- × 5-inch loaf pan that has been sprayed with nonstick spray. Bake for 1 hour and 10 minutes, until golden and springy to the touch. Cool in the pan on a wire rack.

Makes 1 loaf, with about 16 slices.

PUMPKIN MUFFINS

Divide the batter among 12 muffin cups that have been sprayed with nonstick spray or lined with paper liners; bake at 400°F for 20–25 minutes, until golden and springy to the touch.

Irish Soda Bread

I'm always amazed that people don't make Irish soda bread more often—it's such an easy way to have freshly baked bread in no time at all! This recipe is perfect if you're not inclined to attempt yeast bread from scratch—success is pretty much guaranteed.

2 cups all-purpose flour

2 cups whole wheat flour

2 Tbsp brown sugar

2 tsp baking powder

1 tsp baking soda

1 tsp salt

1 large egg

2 cups buttermilk or thin yogurt

flour or old-fashioned oatmeal, for rolling

Per wedge:

Calories	132
Total fat	1 g
saturated fat	0.3 g
monounsaturated fat	0.2 g
polyunsaturated fat	0.2 g
Protein	5.1 g
Carbohydrates	26.1 g
Cholesterol	14.5 mg
Fiber	2.4 g
Calories from fat	7%

1 Preheat oven to 375°F.

2 In a large bowl, combine all the dry ingredients—flour through salt. In a small bowl or measuring cup, stir together the egg and buttermilk with a fork, and add all at once to the dry ingredients. Stir until you have a soft ball of dough. While you're mixing, feel free to add any additions you think would be nice—a handful of dried fruit, nuts, grated cheese, or fresh herbs.

3 Sprinkle your countertop with a little flour or oats and knead the dough about 10 times, shaping it into a ball. Place on a baking sheet that has been sprayed with nonstick spray and cut an X lightly on the top.

4 Bake for 45–55 minutes, until it's golden and sounds hollow when you tap it on the bottom.

Makes 1 loaf, or 16 wedges.

FRUIT & NUT SODA BREAD
Stir ½ cup each dried fruit (such as raisins, cranberries, or chopped apricots) and chopped nuts (such as walnuts or pecans) into the dough.

Apple & Fruit Scones

When you bake with dried fruit, make sure it's plump—fruit that's too dried out will absorb moisture from the batter it's in.

2 cups all-purpose flour

1 cup whole wheat flour

⅓ cup sugar

1 Tbsp baking powder

½ tsp baking soda

¼ tsp salt

¼ cup butter, chilled and cut into bits

½ cup dried fruit, such as cranberries, raisins, and chopped apricots

¼ cup chopped pecans or walnuts (optional)

¾ cup buttermilk

1 large egg

grated zest of 1 orange or lemon (optional)

1 large apple, unpeeled and grated with the coarse side of a box grater

Per scone (based on 12 scones):

Calories	206
Total fat	4.8 g
saturated fat	2.7 g
monounsaturated fat	1.3 g
polyunsaturated fat	0.4 g
Protein	4.8 g
Carbohydrates	37 g
Cholesterol	28.8 mg
Fiber	2.6 g
Calories from fat	21%

1. Preheat oven to 400°F.

2. In a large bowl combine the flours, sugar, baking powder, baking soda, and salt. Using a pastry blender, whisk, or fork, add the butter and work it in until the mixture is well blended and crumbly. (Alternatively, you could do this part in the food processor, then transfer the mixture to a bowl.) Stir in the dried fruit and, if you like, the nuts.

3. In a small bowl, stir together the buttermilk, egg, and, if you like, the orange zest. Add to the flour mixture along with the grated apple and stir just until you have a soft dough.

4. To make round scones, pat the dough about ¾ inch thick on a lightly floured surface and cut with a biscuit cutter, glass rim, or the open end of a can. Place on a baking sheet that has been sprayed with nonstick spray. For wedges, pat the dough into a 1-inch-thick circle on a baking sheet that has been sprayed with nonstick spray; cut into 8 wedges, and pull them apart, spacing them about 1 inch from each other on the sheet. If you like, brush the tops with a little milk and sprinkle with sugar. Bake for 20–30 minutes, until golden.

Makes 8–12 scones.

Jelly Fauxnuts

Ever since I was a kid I've had a weakness for jelly donuts. These rich and cakey muffins are filled with jam and topped with sugar like jelly doughnuts, but then baked instead of deep-fried. This is a great basic muffin recipe to have—instead of filling them with jelly, you can stir in berries, chopped or dried fruit, grated carrots, zucchini or cheese, nuts, citrus zest—think of it as a blank muffin canvas. If you don't have buttermilk, use regular milk, a tablespoon of baking powder, and no baking soda.

2 cups all-purpose flour

½ cup sugar

2 tsp baking powder

½ tsp baking soda

½ tsp salt

1 cup buttermilk

3 Tbsp canola oil

1 large egg

2 tsp vanilla

¼ cup jam, any kind you like

extra sugar, for sprinkling (optional)

Per muffin:

Calories	206
Total fat	5.1 g
saturated fat	0.6 g
monounsaturated fat	2.7 g
polyunsaturated fat	1.4 g
Protein	4.1 g
Carbohydrates	35.7 g
Cholesterol	22.4 mg
Fiber	0.9 g
Calories from fat	22%

1   Preheat oven to 400°F.

2   In a large bowl stir together the flour, sugar, baking powder, baking soda, and salt. In a smaller bowl stir together the buttermilk, oil, egg, and vanilla. Add to the flour mixture and stir gently just until blended. Don't overmix, or the muffins could turn out tough.

3   Line a muffin pan with paper liners or spray them with nonstick spray. (These tend to stick to paper liners until they are completely cool.) Put a big spoonful of batter into each cup, make a little dent in the middle and fill it with about a teaspoon of jam. Put another spoonful of batter on top, covering the jam completely. If you like, sprinkle the tops with sugar.

4   Bake for about 20 minutes, until golden and springy to the touch. Tip the muffins in their cups to help them cool.

Makes about 10 muffins.

CHEESECAKE MUFFINS
Put a small chunk of cream cheese beside the jam in each muffin.

CRUMB CAKES
Omit the jam altogether. Stir 2 tsp cinnamon into ¼ cup sugar to make cinnamon-sugar, then sprinkle the half-filled muffin cups with half the cinnamon-sugar, top with the remaining batter, and then sprinkle with the remaining cinnamon-sugar.

Chocolate Cake or Cupcakes with Marshmallow Frosting

This is a great basic chocolate cake recipe to have—it's rich, dark, almost chewy, but not too sweet—and makes a great Bundt cake (you can eat in plain wedges with your fingers) or cupcakes. It is adapted from one I found in an old issue of *Eating Well* magazine. The Fluffy White Frosting is a perfect pairing—light and marshmallowy and easily tinted with food coloring if need be.

2 cups all-purpose flour

1 cup sugar

¾ cup cocoa

1½ tsp baking powder

1½ tsp baking soda

½ tsp salt

1¼ cups buttermilk

¾ cup packed brown sugar

2 large eggs or 3 large egg whites

¼ cup canola oil

2 tsp vanilla

1 cup strong coffee, cooled

Fluffy White Frosting (optional)

2 large egg whites

1½ cups sugar

¼ tsp cream of tartar (optional)

1 Tbsp light corn syrup

⅓ cup water

1 Preheat oven to 350°F.

2 In a large bowl, combine flour, sugar, cocoa, baking powder, baking soda, and salt. Add buttermilk, brown sugar, eggs, oil, and vanilla and beat for 1–2 minutes, until well blended and smooth. Beat in the coffee. The batter will be thin.

3 Pour into a Bundt pan that has been sprayed with nonstick spray or into cupcake tins that have been lined with paper liners. Bake for 45 minutes (Bundt) or 25 minutes (cupcakes), until the top is springy to the touch.

4 To make the frosting, combine the egg whites, sugar, cream of tartar (if using), corn syrup, and water in a large stainless steel or glass bowl, or in the bowl of a double boiler. Place the bowl over a pot with about an inch of boiling water in it, and beat on high speed with an electric mixer for 7–8 minutes, until stiff peaks form. Remove the bowl from the heat immediately.

5 Allow the cake or cupcakes to completely cool before spreading with the frosting.

Serves 16 (Bundt) or makes 2 dozen cupcakes.

Per serving of cake:

Calories	195
Total fat	4 g
saturated fat	0.5 g
monounsaturated fat	2.2 g
polyunsaturated fat	1.1 g
Protein	3.7 g
Carbohydrates	38 g
Cholesterol	0.7 mg
Fiber	2.4 g
Calories from fat	18%

Per cupcake:

Calories	130
Total fat	2.7 g
saturated fat	0.4 g
monounsaturated fat	1.5 g
polyunsaturated fat	0.7 g
Protein	2.5 g
Carbohydrates	25.3 g
Cholesterol	0.4 mg
Fiber	1.6 g
Calories from fat	18%

ZUCCHINI CHOCOLATE CAKE
Stir in 1 medium zucchini, unpeeled, and coarsely grated, along with the coffee.

Spiced Tomato-Apple Cake

Ever heard of tomato soup cake? This moist, dense cake makes use of tomato paste instead, which is a concentrated form of lypocene and naturally very sweet—after all, a tomato is a fruit! The result is a mildly spiced cake you can eat, like an apple, out of hand.

1½ cups all-purpose flour

1½ cups whole wheat flour

2 Tbsp ground flax seeds (optional)

1 Tbsp baking powder

2 tsp cinnamon

½ tsp salt

4 tart apples, unpeeled and cut into large (½- to 1-inch) chunks

1 Tbsp lemon juice (or enough to keep them from turning brown)

2 large eggs + 2 large egg whites

½ cup canola or olive oil

1 cup packed brown sugar

½ cup sugar

one 5½ oz can tomato paste

empty tomato paste can full of orange juice or water (about half a cup)

2 tsp vanilla

½–1 cup chopped walnuts or pecans (optional)

Per slice:

Calories	176
Total fat	5.3 g
saturated fat	0.5 g
monounsaturated fat	2.9 g
polyunsaturated fat	1.5 g
Protein	3 g
Carbohydrates	30.2 g
Cholesterol	18 mg
Fiber	2 g
Calories from fat	26%

1. Preheat the oven to 350°F. Spray a Bundt or tube pan well with nonstick spray.

2. In a large bowl, stir together the flours, ground flax seeds (if using), baking powder, cinnamon, and salt. In another bowl, toss the apple chunks with lemon juice, about ¼ cup of the sugar, and a bit of cinnamon; set aside.

3. In a third bowl, whisk together the eggs, egg whites, oil, brown sugar, sugar, tomato paste, orange juice, and vanilla until smooth. Add to the dry ingredients and stir just until blended.

4. Pour a third of the batter into the prepared pan and smooth the top. Scatter with a third of the apples (and half the nuts, if you're using them), then repeat with another layer of batter and apples and nuts, and a final layer of batter, then apples. (Nuts are best kept inside the cake to keep them from burning.) Pour any juices that accumulated in the bottom of the apple bowl overtop.

5. Bake for 1 hour and 10 minutes, until golden and springy to the touch. Cool the cake in the pan to lukewarm before inverting it onto a wire rack or plate.

Makes 1 cake; serves 24.

Berry, Peach, Apple, or Plum Crumble Cake

This buttery cake wins the Miss Congeniality award by virtue of ease and accessibility of ingredients. It will enable you to turn a handful of berries or a few humble pieces of fruit into a comforting snack or dessert in about 5 minutes. The fruit possibilities are endless—during the summer, peaches and plums are fantastic. During the holidays, scatter a few fresh cranberries over sliced apples or even pears and grate a little orange zest into the batter. If you're in a hurry and don't want to bother with the crumble, just sprinkle a little sugar over the fruit before you pop it into the oven.

Cake

2 Tbsp butter, melted, or canola or olive oil

½ cup sugar

1 large egg

1 tsp vanilla

1 cup all-purpose flour

1 tsp baking powder

¼ tsp salt

½ cup milk, buttermilk, or plain yogurt

1–2 cups fresh or frozen (not thawed) berries, or 2 peaches or apples, or 3–4 plums

Crumble

⅓ cup whole wheat or all-purpose flour

⅓ cup packed brown sugar

½ tsp cinnamon (optional)

2 Tbsp butter or canola oil

2 Tbsp honey or maple syrup

¼ cup sliced almonds (optional)

Per serving:

Calories	201
Total fat	3.5 g
saturated fat	1.9 g
monounsaturated fat	1 g
polyunsaturated fat	0.3 g
Protein	3.2 g
Carbohydrates	39.5 g
Cholesterol	31.4 mg
Fiber	1.2 g
Calories from fat	15%

1. Preheat oven to 350°F.

2. For the cake, beat the butter and sugar in a medium bowl until well blended; beat in the egg and vanilla.

3. In a small bowl, stir together the flour, baking powder, and salt. Add half to the butter mixture and stir by hand just until combined. Stir in the milk, then add the remaining flour mixture and stir just until blended. If you're using peaches, apples, or plums, slice them as thick or as thin as you like, with or without peeling them (I don't).

4. Spread the batter into an 8- × 8-inch pan that has been sprayed with non-stick spray. Sprinkle the berries overtop or layer the sliced fruit on top, placing the slices close together or overlapping them; fruit shrinks as it cooks, so don't worry about crowding.

5. For the crumble, in a small bowl stir together the flour, brown sugar, cinnamon (if using), butter, and honey with a fork or your fingers until it's well blended and crumbly. Stir in the almonds and sprinkle over the fruit, squeezing it into clumps as you go.

6. Bake for 30–40 minutes, until golden and springy to the touch. Cool in the pan on a wire rack.

Serves 9.

Salad Bars

Necessity is the mother of invention, as evidenced every August when I end up with armloads of zucchini. (Not because I grow it or have particularly generous neighbors, but because it's cheap.) In an attempt to use up my stash, I'd make a carrot-zucchini cake and add a dollop of tomato to add moisture and a vitamin boost. The result would be a deliciously moist cake that was perfect topped with lemony cream cheese frosting. No one would ever guess these low-fat, cakey bars have three kinds of veggies in them!

3 Tbsp butter or nonhydrogenated margarine, softened

¾ cup packed brown sugar

1 large egg

1 tsp vanilla

1 cup all-purpose flour, or half all-purpose, half whole wheat

1 tsp baking soda

½ tsp cinnamon

¼ tsp salt

pinch allspice

1 small zucchini, unpeeled and grated

1 carrot, peeled and grated

2 Tbsp tomato paste

½ cup raisins or dried cranberries

¼ cup chopped pecans or walnuts

Cream Cheese Frosting (optional)

¼ cup light cream cheese, softened

1 Tbsp lemon juice or water

1½ cups icing sugar

1. Preheat oven to 350°F.

2. In a large bowl, beat the butter, brown sugar, egg, and vanilla until smooth. In a small bowl, combine the flour, baking soda, cinnamon, salt, and allspice.

3. Add the flour mixture to the egg mixture along with the grated zucchini, carrot, tomato paste, raisins, and pecans and stir by hand just until combined. Spread the batter in an 8- × 8-inch pan that has been sprayed with nonstick spray.

4. Bake for 25–30 minutes, until golden and springy to the touch. Cool in the pan on a wire rack.

5. To make the cream cheese frosting, beat the cream cheese until fluffy. Add the lemon juice and icing sugar and beat until smooth. Add a little extra sugar or lemon juice if you need it to achieve a spreadable consistency. Wait until the cake cools to frost it and cut into bars.

Makes 12 bars.

Per bar (with frosting):

Calories	233
Total fat	5.9 g
saturated fat	2.6 g
monounsaturated fat	2.2 g
polyunsaturated fat	0.6 g
Protein	2.7 g
Carbohydrates	44 g
Cholesterol	28.8 mg
Fiber	1.4 g
Calories from fat	22%

Two-Bite Brownies

At only 2 grams of fat per pop, these will satisfy your need for chewy brownies. Be careful not to overbake them—they should be slightly puffed but still soft to the touch. Freeze leftovers and serve them frozen or warmed in the microwave with vanilla ice cream and chocolate syrup. (If you don't have mini muffin cups, the batter can be baked in an 8- × 8-inch pan at 350°F for 25–30 minutes.)

¼ cup butter, softened

1¼ cups sugar

2 large eggs

1 tsp vanilla

1 tsp instant espresso or coffee, dissolved in 1 tsp water

1 cup all-purpose flour

½ cup cocoa

¼ tsp baking powder

¼ tsp salt

Per brownie:

Calories	82
Total fat	2.1 g
saturated fat	1.3 g
monounsaturated fat	0.6 g
polyunsaturated fat	0.1 g
Protein	1.2 g
Carbohydrates	15.5 g
Cholesterol	5.2 mg
Fiber	1 g
Calories from fat	22%

1. Preheat oven to 350°F.

2. In a large bowl, mix together butter and sugar until well combined. Add eggs, vanilla, and coffee and stir until well blended and smooth.

3. In a medium bowl, combine flour, cocoa, baking powder, and salt. Add to the egg mixture and stir by hand just until combined.

4. Spoon the batter into mini muffin cups that have been sprayed with nonstick spray. Bake for 12–15 minutes, until puffed but still soft to the touch. Do not overbake! Cool in the pan on a wire rack.

Makes 2 dozen brownies.

Sweet Eats

Everyone needs a little something sweet sometimes. Fudge is good for the soul. Peanut brittle always makes me happy. We eat for many reasons that have nothing to do with nutrition, and that's okay—so long as Ben & Jerry haven't become your closest friends.

All of the sweets in this chapter will satisfy a sweet tooth with less fat than traditional desserts. If you're a chocoholic, don't think you have to go without—chocolate contains the same antioxidants as red wine and green tea, and the darker the better. If you're a purist, chocolate that contains over 60% cocoa is the best choice. When you need some, indulge in a small piece of the very best chocolate you can find—there's no substitute for the real thing.

Chocolate Panini

These were inspired by the chunks of chocolate stuffed into wedges of fresh baguette I saw kids eating after school in Europe, and of course by chocolate croissants. These are far lower in fat, and contain healthier fats, if you brush the bread with canola oil. They are perfect for a party any time of day. If you don't have a panini grill you can cook them in a hot frying pan, weighed down with another frying pan on top to press them down as they cook.

1 baguette, white, sourdough, or whole wheat

one 3.5 oz bar dark chocolate (such as Lindt 70% cocoa)

2 Tbsp canola oil, or as much as you need for brushing

Per panini:

Calories	132
Total fat	7.3 g
saturated fat	2.7 g
monounsaturated fat	1.8 g
polyunsaturated fat	0.9 g
Protein	2.4 g
Carbohydrates	13.7 g
Cholesterol	0 mg
Fiber	1.2 g
Calories from fat	50%

1. To make chocolate panini, all you need is a good baguette and a bar or two (depending on how many you want to feed) of dark chocolate—I buy the 3.5 oz bars of Lindt 70% cocoa because the large, flat squares work perfectly in a panini. (And of course when it comes to chocolate, the darker the better in terms of antioxidants.)

2. Slice the baguette thinly on a slight diagonal. I like to make one slice through, then one almost through, then another through, creating little bread pockets—with just 2 slices still attached at one end—so I can tuck a piece of chocolate in and not worry about the layers sliding around. Brush both sides with a bit of canola oil (or spread with soft butter, or leave them plain) and cook in a panini grill until crispy and golden and the chocolate is melted. If you don't have a panini grill, you can cook them in a hot frying pan, weighed down with another frying pan on top (and maybe a can set in the frying pan) to press them down as they cook.

Makes 10 panini.

Chocolate Fudge

Who doesn't adore fudge? Unfortunately, fudge is generally high in fat, sugar, and calories, but after much experimentation I came up with a formula for rich chocolate fudge with hardly any fat. Cocoa is a great ingredient to use if you're watching your fat intake—it contains all of the chocolate flavor and virtually none of the fat.

2 cups sugar

⅓ cup cocoa

¼ tsp salt

⅔ cup 2% milk

2 Tbsp corn syrup

2 Tbsp butter

1 tsp vanilla

⅓ cup chopped walnuts or pecans (optional)

Per serving:

Calories	167
Total fat	2.3 g
saturated fat	1.4 g
monounsaturated fat	0.7 g
polyunsaturated fat	0.1 g
Protein	0.9 g
Carbohydrates	38 g
Cholesterol	5.7 mg
Fiber	1.1 g
Calories from fat	12%

1 Combine the sugar, cocoa, salt, milk, and corn syrup in a heavy saucepan set over medium heat. Cook, stirring constantly, until the sugar dissolves. Bring to a boil and cook until the mixture reaches 234°F on a candy thermometer. Remove from the heat and add the butter and vanilla, but don't stir it—let it sit until it cools to 110°F.

2 Stir vigorously until the mixture loses its gloss (stir in a handful of nuts at this point if you like), and quickly spread into an 8- × 8-inch pan or a loaf pan that is either nonstick or has been lined with parchment or foil. Cool until set.

Makes 1 pound; serves about 12.

Sponge Toffee

This was my favorite treat (okay, one of many) when I was a kid—my mom would buy little blocks of sponge toffee for my sisters and me when she went to the little grocery store by our house. It's also known as Sea Foam Candy or Cinder Toffee and can be served straight up or dipped in melted chocolate. True, this doesn't have any nutritional value, but at least it's fat free and really delicious. When I'm craving something sweet, a little chunk of sponge toffee always does the trick. Keep in mind it's not the best recipe to make with kids, as the sugar mixture gets dangerously hot.

¾ cup sugar

¼ cup corn syrup

1 Tbsp baking soda

Per serving:

Calories	82
Total fat	0 g
saturated fat	0 g
monounsaturated fat	0 g
polyunsaturated fat	0 g
Protein	0 g
Carbohydrates	21.2 g
Cholesterol	0 mg
Fiber	0 g
Calories from fat	0%

1   Spray a 9- × 13-inch pan really well with nonstick spray.

2   Combine the sugar and syrup in a medium-sized heavy saucepan set over medium-low heat. (Make sure there is lots of room in the pan for the mixture to foam up when you stir in the baking soda.) Stir until the sugar begins to melt. Continue to cook, swirling the pan occasionally but not stirring, until the mixture turns a deep caramel color. Watch it carefully—sugar can burn quickly!

3   Remove from heat and quickly stir in the baking soda. It will foam up like a science experiment! Quickly pour it into the pan and set aside until it has set, which takes a couple hours. To serve, break it into chunks.

Serves 10.

Sesame Snaps

When I was little, sesame snaps and sponge toffee were my favorite treats to get when we went to the grocery store. You can still buy the same little blue and white packages of it by the check-out, but homemade is easy and much tastier. This recipe can easily be halved or doubled.

½ cup sugar

½ cup honey or Rogers' Golden Syrup

½ cup sesame seeds

Per piece:

Calories	59
Total fat	1.5 g
saturated fat	0.2 g
monounsaturated fat	0.6 g
polyunsaturated fat	0.7 g
Protein	0.6 g
Carbohydrates	11.7 g
Cholesterol	0 mg
Fiber	0.3 g
Calories from fat	22%

1 Combine the sugar and honey in a medium-large heavy saucepan. Stir over medium heat until the sugar dissolves. Continue to cook without stirring until the caramel turns light golden, swirling the pan occasionally. Add the sesame seeds and continue to cook in the same manner until the mixture turns deep golden. Watch it carefully—sugar can burn quickly!

2 Pour the mixture onto a baking sheet that has been sprayed with nonstick spray or lined with a Silpat mat. Imme-diately tilt the pan to make it spread as thin as possible—do it quickly because the edges begin to cool first. If you need help, use the back of a spoon that has been rubbed with a little oil.

3 Set it aside to cool. Once it has cooled, break into chunks. Store in a tightly sealed container, especially if you live somewhere humid!

Makes about 2 dozen 2-inch pieces.

Divinity

Divinity is like a cross between meringue and nougat, with the look and texture of thick icing until it sets and dries, at which point it becomes dense and chewy. The only fat it contains comes from the pecans; try stirring in some chopped chocolate instead (or as well as), or leave it plain. This keeps very well and is great for shipping, as it's not fragile and won't bash around in the box.

2⅔ cups sugar

⅔ cup light corn syrup

½ cup water

2 large egg whites

1 tsp vanilla

½ cup chopped pecans, walnuts, or other nuts, toasted

Per piece:

Calories	129
Total fat	1.5 g
saturated fat	0.1 g
monounsaturated fat	0.9 g
polyunsaturated fat	0.4 g
Protein	0.5 g
Carbohydrates	29.5 g
Cholesterol	0 mg
Fiber	0.1 g
Calories from fat	10%

1 Line a couple baking sheets with waxed or parchment paper.

2 In a large, heavy saucepan, combine the sugar, corn syrup, and water over medium heat; stir until sugar is dissolved. Cook without stirring, swirling the pan occasionally, until the mixture reaches 260°F (hard-ball stage) on a candy thermometer, or until a small amount dropped into a bowl of ice water forms a hard ball that holds its shape but is still pliable.

3 In a large bowl, beat the egg whites with an electric mixer until stiff peaks form. Pour in the hot syrup in a thin stream, beating constantly, then add the vanilla. Continue to beat until the mixture loses its gloss and holds its shape—it should take around 10 minutes in total. Stir in the nuts.

4 Drop the mixture in spoonfuls onto the prepared sheet and let cool at room temperature for several hours, until firm and dry. Store in an airtight container.

Makes about 2 dozen pieces.

COCONUT DIVINITY
Add ½ cup shredded coconut in place of the nuts, and use coconut extract instead of vanilla.

PEPPERMINT DIVINITY
Add ½ cup crushed candy canes or hard peppermint candies in place of the nuts, and peppermint extract instead of vanilla.

My Grandma's Peanut Brittle

The recipe for my grandma's peanut brittle is written by hand on an old recipe card I still have; it turns out to make a great basic recipe whether you want to make a nut brittle with peanuts, hazelnuts, almonds, pecans, or mixed nuts. Try crushing nut brittle and stirring it into cookie dough or swirling it into softened ice cream.

1½ cups sugar

½ cup corn syrup or honey

pinch salt

¾ cup water

1½–2 cups dry roasted peanuts or mixed nuts

1 tsp vanilla

1 tsp baking soda

Per serving:

Calories	293
Total fat	10.9 g
saturated fat	1.5 g
monounsaturated fat	5.4 g
polyunsaturated fat	3.4 g
Protein	5.2 g
Carbohydrates	47.1 g
Cholesterol	0 mg
Fiber	1.9 g
Calories from fat	32%

1 Combine the sugar, corn syrup, salt, and water in a saucepan and bring to a boil over medium-high heat. Stir constantly until the sugar dissolves. Once the sugar has dissolved do not stir, but swirl the pan occasionally until the mixture reaches 325°F (caramel stage) on a candy thermometer.

2 Remove from heat and stir in the peanuts, vanilla, and baking soda—the mixture will foam up in the pan. Immediately pour onto a rimmed baking sheet that has been sprayed with nonstick spray and spread out fairly thin with a spatula or the back of a spoon that has been sprayed as well.

3 Cool completely and break into chunks. Store in an airtight container for up to 2 weeks.

Makes about 10 servings.

HAZELNUT OR ALMOND BRITTLE
Replace the peanuts with toasted hazelnuts or sliced almonds.

CHOCOLATE-NUT BRITTLE
Add ¼ cup sifted (just to get rid of the lumps) cocoa powder along with the baking soda.

PUMPKIN SEED BRITTLE
Replace the peanuts with toasted, salted pumpkin seeds; if you like, add a pinch of ground cumin too.

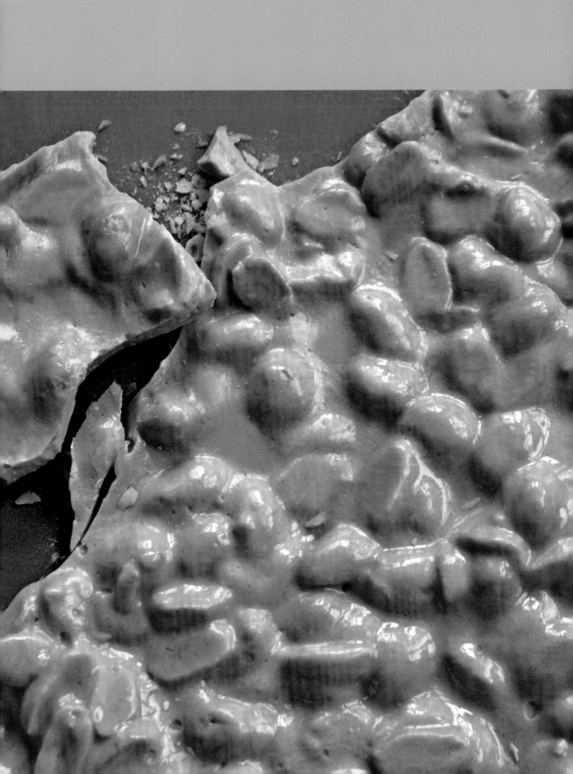

Quickies

Let's face it—we don't always have time to plan ahead. But there's no need to panic when you have to come up with something delicious in a hurry. With a few quick and easy ideas up your sleeve, you can toss out all those take-out menus and stop spending money on packaged snacks. This is real fast food!

If you are what you eat, I'm usually fast, cheap, and easy . . .

ROASTED SPICED PUMPKIN SEEDS

Wash about 2 cups fresh pumpkin seeds and dry them well with paper towels (this is important if you want them to be crisp). Toss in a bowl with 1–2 Tbsp canola or olive oil; 1 tsp salt; ½ tsp each chili powder, curry powder, and cumin; and a grind of black pepper. Spread in a single layer on a rimmed baking sheet and roast at 400°F for 20–30 minutes, stirring occasionally, until golden and crisp.

SALTED OR SPICED EDAMAME

Boil fresh or frozen edamame for about 5 minutes, or until tender. Drain well and sprinkle generously (in their pods) with coarse salt, and if you like them spicy, ½–1 tsp chili powder.

BAKED TORTILLA CHIPS

To make tortilla chips, simply cut fresh flour tortillas (page 41) into wedges (this is easy to do in quantity if you stack them first) and bake on a baking sheet at 350°F for 10 minutes, or until crisp.

CINNAMON-SUGAR TORTILLA CHIPS

Lightly beat an egg white with 1 Tbsp water and brush it over flour tortillas (page 41); sprinkle with cinnamon-sugar. Cut into wedges and bake on a baking sheet at 350°F for 10 minutes, or until crisp.

CHILI-LIME CORN CHIPS

Brush fresh corn tortillas with lime juice and sprinkle with coarse sea salt, chili powder, and cumin. Cut into wedges and bake on a baking sheet at 350°F for 10 minutes, or until crisp.

CHEWY BREADSTICKS

Twist pretzel (page 157) or pizza dough (page 115) or thawed frozen bread dough into elegant breadsticks as long or short as you like. Make them fairly thin, place on a baking sheet and brush with a little egg white or oil, then sprinkle with salt or other seasonings. Bake at 350°F for about 15 minutes, until golden.

ROASTED RED PEPPER & FETA DIP

Purée 2 roasted red peppers with ½ cup crumbled feta and a couple tablespoons of olive oil; if you like, add a couple tablespoons of pine nuts as well. Refrigerate for at least a couple hours to allow flavors to blend.

BUTTERMILK-PEPPERCORN DIP

Stir together 1 cup low-fat sour cream, ½ cup buttermilk, 1 finely chopped shallot (or a bit of dehydrated onion), 1 tsp freshly ground black pepper, and ½ tsp salt; serve with veggies for dipping.

CRANBERRY-ORANGE GOAT CHEESE SCHMEAR

Blend an 8 oz tub light spreadable cream cheese with ½ cup soft goat cheese, the grated zest of an orange, ¼ cup dried cranberries, and 1 Tbsp honey, or to taste. Spread on mini bagels.

GREEK MINI PITA POCKETS

Spread halved mini pitas with hummus and tuck in some roasted chicken, leftover lamb, a lamb meatball (page 129), or crumbled feta; add some thinly sliced purple onion, diced tomato, and a few sprigs of spring greens.

MEDITERRANEAN MINI PITAS

Spread mini pitas with hummus; sprinkle with chopped roasted red peppers, black olives, torn fresh basil, and crumbled feta. Bake at 400°F for 5 minutes.

MINI CALIFORNIA PIZZAS

Spread mini pitas thinly with pesto; top with cooked shrimp, snipped sun-dried tomatoes, and crumbled feta. Bake at 400°F for 5–7 minutes.

PROSCIUTTO PRAWNS

Wrap uncooked tail-on prawns with half a thin slice of prosciutto and grill or cook in a hot frying pan with a little oil for 2–3 minutes, just until pink and opaque. Serve with bottled pesto for dipping.

OLIVE DEVILED EGGS

Make deviled eggs by mashing half the cooked yolks with heart-healthy Olive Tapenade (page 79); return to the cooked, halved egg whites and sprinkle with chopped parsley.

SALAMI CHIPS

Lay thin slices of salami in a single layer on a baking sheet; cover with parchment, then another layer of salami and parchment if you like. Bake at 350°F for 15–20 minutes, until crispy and most of the fat has been rendered. Blot with a paper towel. Peel from the parchment and serve warm.

ROASTED RED PEPPER QUESADILLAS

Sprinkle crumbled feta or goat cheese, chopped roasted red pepper, and chopped black olives between 2 flour tortillas (page 41) and grill or cook in a dry frying pan until golden and crispy on both sides and the cheese is melted.

REFRIED BEAN QUESADILLAS

Spread canned refried beans or mashed kidney beans, grated old cheddar or Monterey Jack cheese, and, if you like, a bit of chopped fresh cilantro between 2 flour tortillas (page 41) and grill or cook in a dry frying pan until golden and crispy on both sides and the cheese is melted.

SUN-DRIED TOMATO, PESTO, SHRIMP & FETA MINI PIZZAS

Spread mini pitas with basil pesto; sprinkle with chopped sun-dried tomatoes, chopped cooked shrimp, and crumbled feta cheese. Bake at 350°F for 15–20 minutes, until golden.

CRUNCHY RAVIOLI-ON-A-STICK

Boil ravioli, tortellini, or other filled pasta, drain well, and roll in dry breadcrumbs and Parmesan cheese to coat. Heat a bit of oil in a nonstick frying pan and cook the pasta for a couple minutes per side, until golden. Thread on a bamboo skewer alone or with a meatball, and serve with tomato sauce for dipping.

STICKY PEACH-CHICKEN SKEWERS

Stir together 1 cup peach jam or chutney, ½ cup barbecue sauce, a small grated onion, and 2 Tbsp soy sauce; marinate bite-sized chunks of chicken breast or thigh and thread the pieces onto bamboo skewers. Grill or broil for a few minutes, just until cooked through.

PEANUT SATAY

Mix ¼ cup each barbecue sauce, peanut butter, and soy sauce and use it to marinate a pound of chicken, pork, or beef strips. Thread onto soaked bamboo skewers and grill or broil for a few minutes per side, just until cooked through. Simmer any remaining marinade in a small saucepan or in the microwave to cook it through and serve alongside for dipping.

SHRIMP WITH ORANGE-CHILI HOISIN SAUCE

Mix ¾ cup bottled hoisin sauce, ¼ cup thawed orange juice concentrate, and a squirt of red chili paste; serve with chilled cooked tail-on shrimp for dipping.

STUFFED MUSHROOMS

Use thick spreads or tart fillings to stuff mushroom caps; sprinkle with breadcrumbs, and/or a little Parmesan and bake them at 350°F until bubbly.

CURRIED SHRIMP SALAD CUPS

Toss ½ lb cooked baby shrimp (or chopped large shrimp) with ¼ cup light mayonnaise, 2 Tbsp chopped fresh cilantro, 1 Tbsp mango chutney, a squeeze of lime juice, and ½ tsp curry paste. Use it to fill baked wonton cups (page 134) or roll in lettuce leaves.

STICKY BALSAMIC PROSCIUTTO-WRAPPED DATES

Bring ½ cup each balsamic vinegar and water and ¼ cup sugar to a simmer in a saucepan set over medium heat. Add 24 whole pitted dates and simmer for 10 minutes. Wrap each date in a thin slice of prosciutto; place on a baking sheet and brush with any remaining balsamic syrup. Bake at 350°F for 5–10 minutes.

PARMESAN-STUFFED BACON-WRAPPED DATES

Pull the pits out of large Medjool dates and stuff with a small chunk of Parmesan cheese (about the same size as the pit); cut slices of bacon crosswise in thirds and wrap each piece around a stuffed date. Place seam side down on a baking sheet (no need to use toothpicks) and bake at 350°F for 10–20 minutes, or until the bacon is cooked through.

LETTUCE WRAPS WITH FIGS, ROASTED RED PEPPERS & PARMESAN

Arrange the small inner leaves of romaine lettuce on a platter with some sliced fresh or dried figs, sliced roasted red peppers, and fresh Parmesan shavings. Instruct guests to put a little of each in a lettuce leaf, roll it up, and eat.

THAI CHICKEN ROLLS

Scatter flour tortillas (page 41) with chopped roasted chicken, chopped red pepper (raw or roasted), and a handful of bean sprouts; drizzle with peanut sauce and roll them up, tucking in the ends like a burrito, and cut in half diagonally.

TORTILLA CUPS

Cut rounds out of flour tortillas (page 41) with a small cookie cutter. Brush with a bit of oil and press into mini muffin cups; bake at 350°F for about 10 minutes, until golden. Fill with any filling you like—particularly bean-based or Mexican dips.

CHUTNEY GINGERSNAPS

Stir ¼ cup mango chutney and a pinch of cumin into half a package of softened light spreadable cream cheese; spread on small, crisp gingersnaps and top with a second gingersnap.

MEXICAN WONTON PACKETS

Put spoonfuls of Cheesy Black Bean Dip (page 58) or Chorizo Chipotle Dip (page 60) into the middle of wonton wrappers, moisten the edges, fold in half, and press to seal. Brush them with a bit of oil and bake at 400°F for 6–8 minutes, until golden. Serve with guacamole (page 61) or salsa (pages 62–63).

QUICK VEGGIE DIP

Add a few spoonfuls of light mayo and some chopped fresh herbs, curry paste, pesto, chutney, sweet chili sauce, or roasted garlic to plain yogurt or light sour cream for a quick vegetable dip.

SPICY GARLIC-NUT MIX

Sauté 2 crushed cloves of garlic in 1 Tbsp olive or canola oil for a minute, and then stir in ⅔ cup each almonds, peanuts, and cashews. Add 2 tsp each Worcestershire and chili powder and 1 tsp cayenne pepper and cook for a few minutes. Cool and toss with a cup of pretzel sticks and a teaspoon of sea salt.

TOFU-PEANUT SAUCE

Whiz together ½ cup each light peanut butter and silken tofu, 3 Tbsp brown sugar, 2 Tbsp each lime juice and soy sauce, 2 crushed cloves of garlic, and a few drops Tabasco.

JEZEBEL

Stir a tablespoon of Dijon mustard and a teaspoon or two of horseradish into a small jar of apricot or peach preserves, microwave it (you can do it all in the jar) until it's melted, then pour it over a block of light cream cheese or soft goat cheese. Serve with crackers.

ROASTED FETA WITH RED PEPPERS & OLIVES

Broil ½-inch slices of good feta cheese in a shallow gratin dish until golden and bubbly around the edges. Sprinkle with a little oregano and fresh pepper and top with a chopped roasted red pepper, a handful of kalamata olives, and a drizzle of olive oil. Serve with pita chips.

HONEY-ROASTED ONION & GARLIC DIP

Toss 2 chopped onions and a head of peeled garlic cloves with oil and drizzle with honey; roast at 400°F until golden, stirring occasionally. Cool and pulse in a food processor with ½ cup light sour cream, salt, and pepper until chunky. Serve with crackers or potato chips.

EASY BEAN DIP

Combine a can of rinsed and drained kidney beans, a large clove of crushed garlic, 1 Tbsp lime juice, and ½ tsp each chili powder and ground cumin in a food processor and pulse until as chunky or as smooth as you like it.

FRUIT, NUT & CHEESE TRUFFLES

Mix half an 8 oz package light cream cheese with a cup of chopped dried fruit (raisins, golden raisins, cranberries, cherries, and apricots work well), 2 Tbsp orange juice, and a cup of grated old cheddar cheese. Roll into balls and roll in toasted sliced almonds or chopped pecans to coat.

HONEY-ROASTED ALMONDS

Heat ½ cup honey over medium heat until it's very runny; stir in 3 cups whole natural (with their skins, not blanched) almonds and, if you like, 1 tsp cinnamon and a few drops of Tabasco. Spread on a rimmed baking sheet that has been lined with foil, and bake at 300°F for 30–40 minutes, stirring occasionally, until golden.

PEANUT BUTTER & HONEY GORP

Melt ¼ cup light or all-natural peanut butter and ¼ cup honey or maple syrup in the microwave; stir until smooth. Pour over 1 cup dry cereal, 1 cup Teddy Grahams, and 1 cup stick pretzels; spread on a baking sheet and bake at 300°F for 20 minutes. Remove from heat and stir in 1 cup chopped dried fruit; cool.

PEANUT BUTTER & HONEY GRANOLA BITES

Stir together 2 cups low-fat granola (page 11), ¼ cup peanut butter, 2 Tbsp honey, and enough milk to hold the mixture together. Roll into bite-sized balls and chill until firm.

STUFFED APRICOTS

Slice open plump dried apricots like a book, and stuff with a mixture of equal parts blue cheese and light cream cheese and a chunk of toasted walnut. Squish them closed again.

CARAMEL APPLES

Melt 25 unwrapped square caramels with 2 Tbsp water over medium-low heat until smooth. Push Popsicle sticks into the stem ends of 6 small apples (the apples that come prepackaged in bags tend to be smaller than those sold by the pound) and dip in the warm caramel to coat. Set on a foil-lined baking sheet or in paper muffin liners and chill until set.

REAL FRUIT GUMMIES
Purée 2 lb of dried fruit (any one kind or a combination) in a food processor with just enough hot water to make it very smooth. Spread about ¼ inch thick on a rimmed nonstick baking sheet and bake at 200°F for several hours or overnight, until the fruit is soft but firm with a gummy texture. Let it cool and cut into squares or little shapes with a small cookie cutter.

FRUIT LEATHER
Purée a few peeled fresh peaches, nectarines, or apricots in a food processor until very smooth. Spread the purée as thinly and evenly as you can on a rimmed baking sheet lined with foil, parchment, or a silicone baking mat. Bake at 200°F for 3–4 hours, until dry and leathery but still slightly tacky. Peel the leather off the pan, cut it into pieces or strips, roll it up against a piece of plastic wrap, and store in an airtight container or Ziploc bag.

SMOOTHIES
Whiz a cup of yogurt, a banana, 1–2 cups fresh or frozen berries, honey to taste, and 1 cup of ice in a blender until smooth. If it's too thick, add some milk or juice. For added protein, add a spoonful of all-natural peanut butter or tofu.

MUD PIE ICE CREAM SANDWICHES
Spread about 2 Tbsp softened light ice cream onto purchased chocolate wafer cookies, drizzle with a little Hershey's chocolate syrup, and top with a second cookie. Roll the edges in finely chopped nuts and freeze until firm.

STRAWBERRY CHEESECAKE BITES
Hollow out large strawberries and fill them with low-fat cream cheese sweetened with honey and a drop of vanilla.

TRAIL MIX
In a bowl combine any quantity of at least 4 of the following items. It's nice to have a combination of dried fruit, nuts, and starch (such as cereal, popcorn, or pretzels). Store in an airtight container or divide into individual Ziploc baggies to keep on hand to grab and go.

Roasted peanuts, toasted almonds, pecan or walnut halves or pieces, toasted hazelnuts, soy nuts, pine nuts, cashews, toasted sunflower seeds, corn nuts, dried wasabi peas, raisins, dried cranberries, dried cherries, sliced dried apricots, sliced dried pears, dried apple slices, banana chips, chocolate chips, M&M's minis, chopped dark chocolate, chocolate-covered peanuts or raisins, mini marshmallows, pretzel sticks, sesame sticks, dry cereal (Cheerios, Mini-Wheats, Shreddies, Chex, Golden crisp, and corn bran all work well), popcorn, crumbled graham crackers, Teddy Grahams, pretzel nuggets, and mini Goldfish Crackers.

Conversion Tables

Volume

¼ tsp	1 mL
½ tsp	2 mL
1 tsp	5 mL
1½ tsp	7.5 mL
2 tsp	10 mL
1 Tbsp	15 mL
2 Tbsp	30 mL
3 Tbsp	45 mL
¼ cup	60 mL
⅓ cup	80 mL
½ cup	125 mL
⅔ cup	160 mL
¾ cup	185 mL
1 cup	250 mL
1¼ cups	310 mL
1½ cups	375 mL
2 cups	500 mL
3 cups	750 mL
4 cups	1 L
5 cups	1.25 L
6 cups	1.5 L
8 cups	2 L
1 pint	500 mL
1 quart	1 L
6 quarts	6 L

Weight

1 oz	30 g
2 oz	60 g
3 oz	90 g
4 oz/¼ lb	125 g
5 oz	150 g
⅓ lb	170 g
6 oz	175 g
½ lb	250 g
10 oz	300 g
12 oz/¾ lb	375 g
1 lb	500 g
1½ lb	750 g
2 lb	1 kg

Temperature

105°F	41°C
110°F	43°C
200°F	95°C
225°F	105°C
234°F	112°C
250°F	120°C
260°F	127°C
275°F	135°C
300°F	150°C
325°F	160°C
350°F	180°C
375°F	190°C
400°F	200°C
425°F	220°C
450°F	230°C

Length

⅛ inch	3 mm
¼ inch	6 mm
½ inch	1 cm
¾ inch	2 cm
1 inch	2.5 cm
1½ inches	4 cm
2 inches	5 cm
3 inches	8 cm
4 inches	10 cm
5 inches	12 cm
6 inches	15 cm
7 inches	18 cm
8 inches	20 cm
9 inches	23 cm
10 inches	25 cm
12 inches	30 cm
13 inches	33 cm
14 inches	35 cm

Cans, jars, and tubs

3 oz can	85 g
4 oz can	120 g
5½ oz can	156 mL
6 oz jar	170 mL
6 oz can	170 g
8 oz package	250 g
10 oz can	284 mL
13 oz can/jar	375 mL
14 oz can	398 mL
19 oz can	540 mL
28 oz can	796 mL

Pan, loaf, and dish sizes

8- × 8-inch pan	20 × 20 cm (2 L) pan
8- × 4-inch loaf pan	20 × 10 cm (1.5 L) loaf pan
9- × 5-inch loaf pan	23 × 12 cm (2 L) loaf pan
9- × 13-inch pan/ casserole dish	23 cm × 33 cm (3.5 L) pan/casserole dish

Index

Note: Recipe variations are not included in this index.